I'M AWESOME

Frontside Ollie, 1996 in Australia.

I'M AWESOME

ONE MAN'S TRIUMPHANT
QUEST TO BECOME THE
SWEETEST DUDE EVER

Jason Ellis

with Mike Tully

itbooks

AN IMPRINT OF HARPERCOLLINS*PUBLISHERS*

I'M AWESOME. Copyright © 2012 by Jason Ellis. All rights reserved. Printed in the United States of America. No part of this book may be used or reproduced in any manner whatsoever without written permission except in the case of brief quotations embodied in critical articles and reviews. For information address HarperCollins Publishers, 10 East 53rd Street, New York, NY 10022.

HarperCollins books may be purchased for educational, business, or sales promotional use. For information please write: Special Markets Department, HarperCollins Publishers, 10 East 53rd Street, New York, NY 10022.

FIRST EDITION

Designed by Richard Oriolo

Library of Congress Cataloging-in-Publication Data has been applied for.

ISBN 978-0-06-209821-4

12 13 14 15 16   OV/RRD   10 9 8 7 6 5 4 3 2 1

I dedicate this book to Stevie DEEBS Ellis,

my mother, Lorraine, my wife, Andrea,

and my kids, Devin and Tiger

AUTHOR'S NOTE

"I have changed the names of some individuals and the identifying features, including physical descriptions and occupations, of other individuals in order to preserve their anonymity. The dialogue has been re-created to the best of my recollection, which can vary given the circumstances of the moment."

That's what the lawyer told me to say. In normal people words, here's what it means:

Everything in this book is true, at least as best as I can remember. Some names and descriptions have been changed, so I don't get sued and so none of my friends stop talking to me. The point is for me to tell my story; not get a bunch of people pissed off, divorced, or arrested.

Also, I don't know about you, but I don't remember exact conversations that happened twenty years ago, or when I was wasted. So a lot of the dialogue is my best re-creation.

CONTENTS

PART FOUR

I'M AWESOME

INTRODUCTION

I'm in Anaheim, California. Backstage, at the House of Blues.

I've been a professional athlete for half my life. But the last few months have been the hardest, most ridiculous training I've ever put myself through. Cutting weight. Starving myself. Sprinting, every day, even though I have arthritis in my ankles and my knees from skateboarding. Breaking my nose sparring, then going right back to the gym the next morning and getting punched in the nose again.

And now I'm standing behind the curtain, waiting for my introduction. My first pro MMA (Mixed Martial Arts) fight. It's Ryan Scheckler's charity event. All of pro skateboarding is here.

One time, back in Australia, there was a party after a skate demo, and a fight broke out. A real bad one. Everyone rushed over to check it out. I headed for the door immediately. I didn't wanna watch. I couldn't.

I hear the crowd laughing at the intro video I filmed yesterday. Laughing at the funny comedian guy everybody's known for the last twenty years.

I wasn't sure they still knew I existed.

One time Tas Pappas wanted a fight. Me and Tas are two of the only skaters that made it out of Australia. He's a scrappy little guy. He was begging me to kick his ass. And I could have. Easy. Nobody understood why I didn't. I never fought. Even when I was wasted.

My intro music blasts through the speakers. Metallica, of course.

My buddy Mayhem applies Vaseline to my face. King Mo is with me, too, smiling like a little kid. Mo just finished bashing my gloves, over and over. Slamming them in a door backstage. At this point, the padding is nonexistent. If someone did that to my gloves, then I'm pretty sure someone did the same thing to the other guy's gloves, too.

And if that's the case, the first guy to touch the other guy's face is guaranteed a knockout.

I don't know how many times I saw my dad punch another man. I can still see so many of them in my mind. My father punching some dude so hard the guy's face changes right in front of me.

Permanently.

Andrea is a few rows back, pregnant with our second kid. My son, Tiger.

Andrea was scared I was gonna get hurt in the ring. Or worse. Naturally. She calmed down—we both calmed down—when I reminded her, there's no way this guy is gonna hurt me worse than I've hurt myself.

Sal Masekela—from the X Games, and from E!—is doing his best Bruce Buffer impression on the ring announcements.

Sal saw me do some shit, back when we used to be roommates on skate tours. One time, in Germany I think, after chugging absinthe, I came back to the hotel in tears, fucked out of my mind. I was hysterical, because I saw some chick at a brothel getting made fun of really bad, and I didn't do anything to stop it. So I was crying to Sal, blathering on about what a sad world we live in. About how I didn't stick up for her. How I didn't act like a man.

The bell rings. Here we go.

There is no way skater Jason would be in a cage fight. No way *any* skater would.

I am thirty-seven years old.

This is good-bye to skateboarding.

Good-bye to everything.

PART ONE

1.

THINGS REALLY SUCKED
WHEN I WAS LITTLE

The first thing I can remember is eating a cigarette, when I was maybe three years old. A whole one. Unlit. I bit into it and started chewing. I have no idea why. Cigarettes don't taste very good, as you might imagine. They burn. I remember trying to get orange juice. Pouring it in my mouth. All over my face. Desperately trying to get rid of that taste.

It was early in the morning, and everyone else was passed out. There must have been a party the night before. Seems like in those days there was always a party the night before. I was on little kid time, up early and walking around, all by myself. I was by myself a lot when I was little. I don't think too many people were really keeping an eye me. Even then, I remember thinking it was a little weird to be left on my own so often. I'm a parent now. I have two kids. And now, I think it was *really* weird.

My dad was twenty when I was born, near Melbourne, Australia. My mum was sixteen. They got divorced a couple years after that. Neither of them was the most responsible person on the planet. My dad had a crazy temper. He got into fights a lot, oftentimes for little to no reason. And after my parents split up, Mum hung out with a series of extremely shady dudes. With all the things she was doing back then, and the people she surrounded herself with, sometimes I can't believe my mother is even still alive. She was a drinker. Both my parents were. I never saw my mum do drugs, but her boyfriends did, in front of me. So who knows what she might have been up to, besides the alcohol. I definitely saw her get extremely wasted. Put it that way.

Not to say that nobody loved me. I think I was a loved child, for sure. I think my father really loved me. And my mother loves me incredibly. All the parties, the drinking, the drugs—everything I was exposed to—it wasn't like either of them was *trying* to neglect their child. Everyone was doing the best they could.

But there was a lot of craziness. One time, when I was about ten, my mother and one of her boyfriends went to a party. For whatever reason, they ended up taking me with them. I'm sure this guy was not too pumped about having a kid around cock-blocking him all night. All the adults were in the back of the house, in the kitchen. I was watching TV in the living room. By myself again. It was about 2:00 A.M., and I was tired, and I told my mum that I wanted to go home. She told me to wait, so I went and watched some more TV. And then her boyfriend came in. He tried being friendly. "Look, Jay," he said, "if you're tired, I can give you something. Something to keep you awake. It's pretty good. You just can't tell your mum about it." I told him no. I never liked the dude.

A son always knows.

My mum came to check on me a bit later, and I ratted him out instantly. "He tried to give me drugs! And he told me not to tell you!" There was a big fight, and then we left. I couldn't wait to tell my dad. I never saw my mum's boyfriend again after that. My dad wasn't around for a while, either. I think he was trying to find the dude. I remember thinking at the time that there was a definite possibility that my dad would end that guy.

To be honest, I didn't think much of it at the time. It was only when I got older that I realized what a big deal it was to offer a child crystal meth. My mother says she saw her old boyfriend not too long ago, and he looked really bad—no teeth and shit like that. Until she saw him, I believed my father might have killed him.

There were always all these weird losers around my mum, lined up, trying to fuck her. Even as a kid I knew what was going on. I hated them. One time, me and my friend were rolling a joint, and one of these guys grabbed all the weed, put it in his mouth, and ate it. "You guys are too young to smoke weed," he said. There was a lot of stupid shit like that. Another time, there were all these drunk guys out in the garage. Just hanging out. Doing nothing. I was there, too. My mum was in the house. I was doing chin-ups, trying to see how many I could do, and this one dude put his hands over my hands so I couldn't get down. I started freaking out. I was crying. "Get off me!" I was probably ten. My dog came to my rescue and bit him, and then he kicked my dog. I ran into the house and told my mum. I was telling the dude, "You better get out of here. I'm gonna call my dad, and then we'll see how tough you are." He barked right back at me. "Fuck you, ya little shit!" He actually got into a verbal altercation with a ten-year-old.

There was another guy. There were *lots* of other guys, but this one I actually liked. He gave me one hundred Matchbox cars, from when he was a kid. Which was quite a score for me at that point. But then one day, I was coming home from school, and I saw him push my mum over in the front yard. Hard. I ran into the garage while he headed into the house. I was really into Bruce Lee, and I had made nunchuckers out of a sawed-off broom handle and a bicycle chain. I had practiced, too. I knew how to use them a little bit. So I grabbed my nunchuckers and came into the kitchen from the garage. The dude turned around and *WHAM!*, I got him clean, right on the forehead. He went down, so now he was on my level. *WHAP!* Another one right on his face. He grabbed me. He was gonna punch me. He reminded me how easy it would be for him to end my life. I again threatened to call in my dad. (Obviously, at that point that was my go-to move.) He threw me on the ground and started yelling at my mum. "You're a fucking idiot! Your kid's a fucking idiot! We're fucking done!" And off he went.

Sometimes I am a little resentful of my mother. To this day, I think, she probably doesn't understand the severity of some of the things I experienced in my childhood. Her idiot boyfriends fucking with me, constantly. Not too long ago, a reporter was writing an article about me for *ESPN* (the magazine), and I was talking with my mum about the guy who offered me meth. She told me, "He was going through a really tough time then." I don't really get angry about anything anymore, especially when it comes to my mum, but that was really, really hurtful to me. *He was going through a tough time? Are you really defending him?* My daughter is six. If someone offered her crystal meth, I would fucking end them. If I couldn't do it myself, I would find someone who knows someone who would. They would die, and I would gladly know that they were murdered because of me. Fuck, if I had taken the meth, *I* could have died.

At the same time, I feel bad for my mum. She was the one who actually said she loved me. She wanted me around. She did the best she could with the circumstances she was in, being so young, and being an alcoholic. That's a disease. That's not your fault. She had to deal with my dad, too. Him fucking everybody. Him leaving her, and moving in with Marn, her best friend. My mother never got over that. To this day, even though my father and my half brother Stevie are both gone, my mother will tell you my stepmother is the lucky one, because she got my dad.

It's weird that a man like my father could have someone that would stick by him, like my mum. Recently, my mother told me, "Your father was the most violent man I have ever met." Maybe he was abused as a kid. I've heard that, over the years. Who knows? And yet I know that my mother would have stayed with him. She'd still be with him now. Why? I couldn't tell you. He was not a very good husband, to put it lightly. But apparently there was no coming back from falling in love with him. It doesn't make sense to me, but he could have had my mother back whenever he wanted her. Crazy as he was, my dad was a special guy, and not just to my mother. The fact that my stepmother has any feeling for him at all—dead or alive—is proof of that.

OTHER THAN EATING THAT CIGARETTE, the only other thing that stands out from when I was really, really young is telling my mum I wanted to move in with my dad. She sat on the couch and said, "How could you do this to me?" I had a hang-up about that for a long time. Like somehow that was *my* fault. I was at most five or six years old when that happened. After that, I pretty much lived with Dad and Marn. All my stuff would be at their house, although my mum always had a room for me, too. And when my dad and Marn moved down the coast about ten miles, to Sandringham, my mum moved there as well, because of me. So I could come and go wherever I wanted.

I don't remember much from before I moved in with my dad. When I think of that time, I just think of darkness, and violence. My mum and dad lived together in St. Kilda, a small beach town on the outskirts of Melbourne. There are a bunch of old English buildings there, but otherwise it's a lot like a smaller version of Venice Beach in Los Angeles. There's a really shitty boardwalk, and pubs and all that. And just like Venice, there's always been a lot of sketchy stuff going on there. I assume that my mum and dad were in that whole St. Kilda scene. Before I moved in with my dad, there was heroin in my life. I'd met more than one junkie at my mum's house. I can recall, at one point, my mum crying in a corner, and some boyfriend saying "Everything's gonna be all right" while he's shooting up in the living room.

My dad moved to Sandringham because that's where my stepmother is from. She had family there. It's not far from St. Kilda, but it's a pretty mellow town. You can make it there. You can have a little suburban life, if that's what you want. So I don't regret the decision to move in with my dad. He probably was the lesser of two evils. Then again, maybe not. I'm still not sure. For most of my life I looked up to my father immensely, but if he was around today, I'd be a little resentful of him, too.

One thing I'm sure of: If I didn't have my father around me, doing the things he did, you wouldn't be reading this book. I wouldn't have accomplished half the things I've done in my life without him. I have this ongoing obsession with proving my manhood, and it has everything to do with him. I had a very manly father, and believe it or not, I'm really not that manly of a dude, at least on the inside. I've always liked jumping shit and dirt bikes and all that, but I wasn't born to be a tough guy. I got into being tough because I wanted to be like my father. For most of my life, I was really just a scared little baby, trying to fool everyone. Just trying to get by.

Oftentimes, to this day, I'll be there fighting MMA, or flying off something on my skateboard, scaring the shit out of myself, and I'm not even sure I'm enjoying it. And I wonder, Is this who I really am? Or is this who I think my father wanted me to be?

Needless to say, I've got issues. Big ones. Some of them help, to be honest. They push me, constantly. They make me make shit happen. But a lot of my issues do not help at all. It's a never-ending roller coaster.

My father had a temper that scared the shit out of me. Permanently. He's *dead* and I'm still scared of him. He never punched me in the face or anything, but he would turn that temper on me all the time. I used to shit my pants a lot, until I was maybe twelve. My daughter went through it for a while. Andrea read up on it, and it turns out it's just a thing some kids go through. So we did our best to help her. Unlike my old man, who would beat the fuck out of me with this wooden spoon. Sometimes the spoon would snap, and he'd keep going with his hands, and I'd be screaming, crying. It was a big deal, at the time.

When you're young, a lot of things are a big deal. Like acne. When I was a teenager, I got a good shot of acne. And I think I am naturally more self-conscious of the way I look than most people. I'm kind of girly in that way. Like a metrosexual, only without all the hair gel. I wanted people to like the way I looked. To like *me*. So back then, pimples fucked with me, massively. *Oh my God, I've got acne! It is very tough, emotionally, to be Jason Ellis today, because of my amazing amounts of acne!*

I've gotten better about it, though. Now? I'm bald. Fuck off.

I was the oldest, so I got whooped the hardest. Dad never hit my half brothers, but numerous times, he flipped me upside down by my leg, and I'd be doing cartwheels trying to get away. I took a few shots along the way. A few kicks, too. I wouldn't say my father was abusive, but he was a big, strong dude with a really crazy temper. If he had been actually trying to hit me, he would have killed me. Good night.

I'm pretty sure my father hit my mother. One time I saw him hold my stepmother down by her hair, in the kitchen, and say, "Don't you ever fucking do that again, all right? Fucking listen to me!" Who knows what she had done. At that point I hated her, but I still remember thinking how uncool it was of my dad to do that to her. But that's how he was. There was this thing that would come over him, and he would just snap and start getting violent. There was nothing worse than him apologizing, and me being too scared to say, "I don't accept your apology." That was the most annoying part of it to me, when he would calm down later.

If you have a temper around your kids, it will rub off. I understand that now. But I also understand that my mother *was* a kid. And my father wasn't much older than that. Sixteen and twenty? You've gotta be kidding me. If I had a kid at sixteen, I would have called the police immediately and said, "Somebody come grab this kid, before it dies."

My dad moved in with Marn straightaway after leaving my mum. That was when I was about four. I moved in with them pretty soon afterward, but then I didn't really like it there either. When I was six or seven, I ran away, down to the park with a sleeping bag. I actually managed to fall asleep for a bit, before I gave up and went back home that same night.

At that point, my dad still drank a lot with his friends. There would be parties. He had a Ferrari that was his pride and joy. He was always in front of the house washing that thing. I remember him in that Ferrari, drunk, in front of someone's house, flying by and hitting the curb, real close to a bunch of people, and then spinning out and doing burnouts, with everybody cheering. Then moments later he's up against a tree, vomiting, from being too drunk. I was standing there watching with everybody else.

It was my stepmother, Marn, that made everyone grow up, starting when my half brother Lee was born. I didn't like him. As far as I was concerned, he was part of my stepmother, and my stepmother was trying to take my dad from me. I'm sure I made Lee's life pretty difficult. I always told him he had a massive head, to try to give him a complex. Marn and I had it out when I was about ten. That was when we officially told each other that we hated each other. "I hate you!" "Oh yeah, well I hate you too!" I remember thinking, *Well, now it's official. Game on. Let's see if I can get you out of the house.* Lee was four or five by then.

Our mutual hatred was long-standing, and my dad didn't help much with that. Marn was a grounded human being—the only grounded person I had ever known, at that point. Even if I hated her for it at the time. We'd all be in the car, and she'd be saying, "Slow down, Steve!" to my dad. And my dad would say, "Shut up, Marn!" And I'd be like, "Yeah, shut up, Marn!" Common sense might have told him that *he* was the one who should probably shut up, but that thought didn't kick in for him. So in a way, he *made* me resent her. The animosity died off when I got older. By the time I went to America to skate, I had stopped hating Marn. I realized that the only rational influence I had on my upbringing came from her, even if I had rebelled against it at the time.

But by the time Marn started cleaning up my dad's act, and making us a real family, I had already seen a lot of shit. I'd seen everybody smoking weed. I'd seen everybody doing way heavier shit than that at my mum's house. And because I'd already seen it all, there was no point in trying to hide it. "Now we don't do that, Jay," they'd say. Fine, sure—but *I've already seen you do it.*

And anyway, the partying still continued at my mum's, if I wanted to go there. There were weird people around the house. Lots of hot drunk chicks. There were always half-finished drinks for me to grab, if I wanted to.

School was never my thing. I got expelled from my first grammar school. It was a private school that my grandmother paid for. My dad's mum, Kathy. She was the first person that spoiled me, because Dad didn't have shit. My grandmother was the brains in the family. She started the family business, Ellistronics. The store that her husband and my dad would eventually run into the dirt.

Things went south at that school when I snapped a fat kid's arm during a heated dispute over a marble. The kid tried to take my snake eye. Unfairly. I was in the right. And those marbles were everything to me—all different swirls, and snakes, and moons and shit. He pushed me, and I'm chasing him, and punching him, and then he tripped and fell onto a bench, and I fell on top of him. He went into shock. And everybody thought I did it on purpose.

Before my dad came to pick me up, the headmaster whipped me, with a cane and with a belt. That guy used to hit me with the belt quite a lot. One time, the belt missed my ass and went around my leg—and mind you, I had the full-on short-ass "ah g'day mate" school shorts on—and I got the whole outline of the buckle on my skin. It turned purple. You could get away with that shit in those days.

I was in the principal's office when my dad arrived. The guy started telling my dad what a terrible child I was, a terrible student, blah blah blah. (I wasn't really a bad kid. I just wasn't paying attention. At all.) And my dad's rebuttal to all this was to say, "You talk to my son like that again and I'll punch your face in, you stupid cunt." He invited the principal to step outside. There were maybe ten kids there to witness this display. They were extremely impressed.

"Come on, Jay. Fuck this school." My dad led me out of there. It was awesome. I had expected all hell to break loose, at my expense, as soon as he got there. It turns out he just was saving that up for the car. "You fucking idiot!" he said, as soon as the door slammed shut. "All you ever do is fuck everything up! You know how much your grandmother paid for you to go to this school?!"

I really didn't mean to break that kid's arm. It just happened. And that was the best marble, the snake eye. You couldn't even buy them. You had to win 'em.

I had to move back in with my mum to go to the next school, Sandy Tech. I was *not* into moving back. Dad was driving me over to her house, and I wouldn't talk to him. Wouldn't even look at him. So he started whipping the car around in circles. This was not a new car, and it was not a sporty car. It was a rickety old wagon. An old MG. Not safe at all. He smoked the tires until I almost couldn't even see him sitting right next to me. When I finally did, he was smiling at me through the smoke, until he made me laugh, too. He did all that just so I wouldn't stay mad at him.

My dad did hire a tutor for me. It was a proper old guy, with a suit and a beard and an office. He was creepy. I remember the guy giving me some test. For whatever reason, I was able to read better when they stuck this blue lens in front of my face, and apparently that sealed it—I was dyslexic. I think being diagnosed as dyslexic just gave me an excuse to fuck off at school even more, because now, it's not my fault. I went to see the tutor for about two years. I gave it a pretty good go. But I just couldn't read. Couldn't spell. I think once the tutor ended, that was it. My parents, and my teachers—they just gave up. I just fucked up at school, all the time. The only classes I ever passed were phys ed and art. I liked both of those, because they were fun, and because I didn't have to read. Although even those went wrong for me. One time, I made a papier-mâché skate ramp in art class, and then some asshole wrecked it, right outside class, in the corridor. Just to make sure I did not have even that one enjoyable hour in my school day.

I didn't have many friends at school. The friends I did have were way older than me. Danny Clapp and Peter Brampton (yup—real name, *Peter Brampton*) lived down the street. Peter had a big nose. He was always hunched over, and he was really insecure. He could never get any dates. Danny was half aborigine, so he was tan and good-looking. He would just slaughter the chicks.

Even though Danny and Peter were a few years older, they weren't the ones that got me started with partying. They didn't even drink or do drugs, at least at the time. Besides, as I've said, if I wanted something to drink, I could just grab it at my mum's house. Hell, there's pictures of me drinking champagne in front of my dad at this big three-day Hells Angels rally. I'm probably about thirteen in those.

That's around the same time when skateboarding really started to become my thing, and inspired me to develop a little bit of my own personal style. Shred Threads were my favorite. They made shorts that actually had the hip pads built in. I would wear those all day, with my knee pads down around my ankles. Converse All-Stars. Punk rock T-shirts. Shit like that. An AC/DC army jacket.

I was the only skater in my class. Everyone else was a bunch of metalheads. I was actually the pussy of the class. My hair was starting to grow out a bit by then. I was the only boy with blond hair, and I was a pretty good-looking guy. So I got my ass kicked a lot. The most legendary moment in my school career was probably the time I got beat up by a bunch of dudes in some cricket nets.

There were maybe five or six of these guys. They were classmates of mine. One of them had already beaten me up before, for saying something smart. I was always a smart-ass. This guy was way bigger than me, and I must have said some smart-ass thing to him again, and whatever it was, it was once again the wrong thing to say to a big, dumb kid. Especially one with big, dumb friends.

They told me they were going to beat me up that day, at lunchtime. They usually gave me a heads-up in the morning, so I would have to sweat it out before it happened. I knew they would be waiting for me. I was in the bike shed, right after cooking class, looking for them through a window. Meanwhile, Jane Cromberg, my first real girlfriend, was walking my bike out for me while I laid low. I did all right with the ladies back then. I made out with a few different ones, in the park after school. I think that had a little bit to do with me getting my ass kicked repeatedly. These guys definitely did *not* have any girlfriends. Anyway, they knocked Jane over, right on top of my bike. I came out to defend her honor, and they all jumped on me. Then into the cricket net I went. I got beat up for a whole lunch break. I just curled up in a ball and they had at it, from bell to bell. It went on for so long, they actually started getting tired. Just to mix things up, I remember one guy started aiming all his kicks directly for my butthole. With me thinking all the while, *Really? Is no one going to stop this?*

I used to cut school all the time. The teachers didn't want me there, and I didn't want to be there, so that worked out for both of us. But when you cut school, you need to find something to do all day. More often than not, I ended up in this one alley, alone. I walked past it last time I was in Australia. It's still there, behind a Boy Scout hall. This particular alley kind of curves, so there's a place in there you can go where no one driving past can see you. Sandringham's a small town, and if somebody spots you—say, another kid's parents—they'll rat you out for sure. I found this spot one time when I was out walking around by myself. I was always out walking around, everywhere. And then even more so when I got into skateboarding. Every night I was out skating by myself.

I wouldn't say I definitely wanted to spend a bunch of time sitting solo in an alley. But then again it wasn't that bad, given my alternatives. When I was in there, I used to kind of disappear into my mind. I'd let my thoughts wander and run all these imaginary scenarios to pass the time. There's always been an entertainer in there, long before radio came along. What I was really doing, more than anything else, was fantasizing about a day when I had a whole bunch of friends around me, and I was cool and accepted. Although if you had stumbled on me at the time, to the untrained eye I'm sure I just looked like a young psychopath in training.

I eventually got kicked out of Sandy Tech, too. Someone taught me how to make a little smoke bomb. I wasn't necessarily a big prankster, but then again it's never been hard to get me interested in some deviant behavior. You put a Ping-Pong ball in aluminum foil, and then you roll it up and heat the whole thing with a lighter. It makes all this smoke. And it stinks really bad, too, which is a nice bonus at that age. So I made a bunch and threw them in the girls' toilets. I was unloading the last of my arsenal when a teacher spotted me. And then one of the smoke bombs landed on a roll of toilet paper and it went up in flames, so I got expelled for setting the girls' bathroom on fire. Which, just like when I broke the fat kid's arm, wasn't what I was trying to do.

At that point I was motivated to keep going with an education, if only so my father didn't disown me. So I continued on to my third school, which was called Dromana. I lasted there a couple more years. But my dad wasn't into school any more than I was. He was the one to say, "It's over. Your grades are fucking terrible. You should just quit and get a job."

And as soon as I turned sixteen, halfway through my second go at Year Eight, that's exactly what I did.

THEN AGAIN, THEY WERE
ALSO KIND OF SWEET

Like a lot of people, probably, I could give you two completely different angles on my childhood, and both would be true, kind of. On the one hand, it was this hellacious experience I couldn't wait to escape from. But there was another side to growing up, too. If I look at it a certain way, my childhood was actually kind of sweet. After my father got married to Marn, I remember thinking that I actually had it better than most kids. We had a nice house. It was a clean life.

With me being from Australia, you might expect that my childhood was this wild-ass Mick Dundee kind of thing. And actually, you'd be spot-on. I lived more like an "Australian" than most people down there did. Your average kid in Australia is just like a kid in America, but I was a straight-up bush boy. I was covered in mud and rabbit shit, because I was out hunting in the bushes, and fucking with snakes, and throwing rocks at lizards. When I was little, my mum says I used to eat rabbit shit. We had a rabbit, and I was on a mission, at all times. Maybe it's a dude thing. Dudes need to test shit out.

A lot of the best memories revolve around my dad. For most of my life, I wanted to be him. Sure, he scared the shit out of me, but he was my boy.

When I was maybe six, he stuck a block on the gas pedal in his truck, so my foot would reach and I could drive. Around that same time, I got a motorbike. A 50cc Italjet. It was blue. My dad held on to the back of it, out in the backyard, because I didn't know how to ride it. I was gonna fly off as soon as humanly possible, and he knew that was my sole intention. When I finally got to ride it in a park down the street, that's what I did. I pinned it, and I bent the handlebars. It wasn't some kind of ballsy move or anything. I just didn't know what I was doing. I panicked and flew off it and smashed into a fence. I think I wrecked the bike right there. After that I went to a Yamaha YZ80. Me and dad both started riding together, around the same time.

Ellistronics, the family business, was taking off. As opposed to the other adults in my life, my grandmother was actually smart. She set the whole thing up. Back then, we weren't talking about computers. The store sold integrated circuits, transformers, and stuff like that. Little plastic shit in a bucket that would make your TV work. My dad worked there, which was the first time he made any money. That's when toys started to come into play. My dad had a couple of other friends that had just bought bikes, and they were all learning how to ride together. They all went out to the bush to learn.

Camping was one of the highlights of my childhood—riding dirt bikes, hunting rabbits, and hanging out with my father. Lee had brought that stuff on, and then that kind of stuff happened even more so when my other half brother, Stevie, came along. The whole family vibe kicked in. Marn pushed my dad to focus on less antisocial behavior.

There *were* some good times there. We *were* sort of a family. Now that there were a couple of kids, my dad and Marn's friends would still drink around us, but there was noticeably less mayhem. There were still plenty of people shooting guns and setting things on fire, but no fighting, for one thing. Nobody was punching each other in the face anymore. Every now and then, my dad would still be a really bad influence. Drinking and driving and all that. But not like he used to. And in fairness, there was a lot more of that going on back then than there is nowadays. To an extent, that was just the way Australia was.

Then again, I can remember times when Marn would have some friends around the house—some of the more civilized, grown-up type of people she started trying to associate with—and I was intensely aware of what a misfit my dad was compared to them. He was a hoodlum. I could just tell, whoever this guy is that's over for dinner, if it's twenty years earlier, my dad would be punching him in the face, strictly on account of what a pussy this guy is. I know for sure that, at least once, one of Dad's old friends punched one of Marn's new friends, late in the evening at one of these get-togethers.

My dad was crazy. Although he preferred to think of himself as a thrill seeker. To give you an example, sometimes this involved leading the cops on extended car chases. On purpose.

At the drop of the hat, Dad would decide to do some hot wheeling. You know, a little bit of the old mad-dogging. And then—*bem! Bem! BEMMMM!*—he'd hoon off and we'd see how far we could get, if not actually escape, from the po-po.

As you might imagine, my father got arrested *a lot*. But he got away a lot, too.

One time, he was out with this friend of his—another thrill seeker, you could say. A guy he grew up with. At this point, they were both fairly accomplished individuals (this was before Ellistronics went bankrupt four or five times), but, when it came down to it, both of them were also very dangerous thugs. Fights in the street. Trips to the hospital. Broken bones.

My father was driving a Holden Commodore—for those who aren't familiar, it was the most obscene engine and suspension you could get your hands on in Australia at that time.

So him and his friend got wasted, hit a bunch of strip clubs, and then they started burning around in the Holden Commodore. Sure enough, the police come around, and then off they go, hotdogging, with this cop chasing after.

The thing is, my dad was a really good driver. A couple times, observing from shotgun position, I witnessed him throw that same car sideways down a street so that it would come out more or less straight on the next road. Like a getaway guy in a Charles Bronson movie. Ballsy shit. I believed that my father may have accidentally invented drifting during one of these episodes, eluding the police, although he refused to take credit.

One time—*one time*—he had lost a race. He thought he had his man beat, until he saw the guy in the rearview, coming up on him, sideways. My father was in awe of what a great driver this other man was. "No matter how fast you are, there's always someone out there faster." That's what he would always tell me. Truly, words to live by.

So anyway, he and his buddy were driving, all the way from the suburbs into the city, and they manage to get away from the cops. And they're hammered, so they think it would be funny to pull over, and wait for the guy that's chasing them to catch up. So that's what they do.

And sure enough, when the cop catches up, it's not just one cop anymore; it's like four of them. Which was great for these two. I mean, now they've got a proper chase on their hands!

Off they go, into the city. And the cops aren't idiots. As he's darting along, my dad is looking down the side streets, where he can see yet more police cars, flanking him on either side.

It might bear repeating at this point that this high-speed, multi-car chase was not motivated by a crime, or any actual purpose. Just some of that good old-fashioned thrill seeking.

So Dad's gunning down the street—turn here, turn there—*Bem! Bem BEMMM!*—skidding sideways—*shhhhhh!*—through an intersection, and then clean into somebody's driveway. Who knows whose house it is. Then, boom!—both of them are out of the car. They toss the keys in the bushes, and off they walk, like nothing happened.

Naturally, they then holed themselves in the nearest strip club. And after a couple of hours of laying low and getting even more wasted, they head back to pick up the car.

And there are cops fucking everywhere. I know—hard to believe—but somehow Melbourne's finest were able to ascertain that, yes, the car in this inconspicuous driveway was indeed the very same Holden Commodore that half the city's squad cars had just been chasing. (One thing that might have helped tip them off: this particular vehicle had ELLISTRONICS written on the door.)

My dad strolls by the scene, and he must have hung around a bit, to admire the mayhem. Because a cop walks right up to him and starts a friendly chat.

"How's it going, mate?"

"Pretty good, mate."

"This is your car, mate, in't it?"

"Nah, mate. Why would you say that?"

Realizing he was dealing with a smooth operator here, the cop cut to the chase. At this point, I should mention that, in those days in Australia, for some strange reason, if you were a certain kind of guy—the kind of guy my father was—from time to time you could, say, lead multiple police cars on a reckless, dangerous car chase across the city, and occasionally they would *not* send you to jail, and *not* ruin your life. Benefit of the doubt, you know? Good on ya, mate.

"Look, I'm not gonna bust you," the cop said. "But we are gonna take your car down to the station. You can come get the keys, if you want. But something tells me you've been doing a little drinking. So if you wanna come by and get 'em in the morning, you can do that too."

So my dad goes back to the strip club and drinks all night. Then, at seven o'clock in the morning, he goes straight to the police station, gets the keys, and drives home.

End of story.

I remember him going to work the next day, pissed. He couldn't believe his bad luck. "I fucking flat spotted the wheels!" he said.

That was the price he paid, I guess, locking it up to get the car into that driveway. If that was me, trust me, fucked-up wheels would have been a bit further down my list of priorities. Somewhere below getting ass-raped in jail, where I would have been thrown immediately for pulling this sort of maneuver.

BY THE TIME I CAN really remember what was going on, my dad had done a massive amount of growing up, but still, not really. When we were camping, he'd be drunk and shooting off tree branches. Him and his friends would race cars and run over signs and poles in the side of the road, smashing their cars up in the process. Ripping things out of the ground. Out in the bush. With me riding shotgun. Imagine seeing that now? Um, excuse me, sir, are you sure you don't want to put your *kids* to bed before you go drag racing and knocking over stop signs?

Some of the crazy friends from the old days were still in the picture. Stan the Man. He was a dangerous guy, a heavy dude with a real quick temper. He was Greek, or maybe Lebanese. He might have killed some people, for all I know. More likely, he just knew a guy who knew a guy. He might have been selling stolen cars. I'm not sure. Stan the Man definitely wasn't paying taxes, put it that way. His girlfriend died in jail. Some other prisoners set her on fire. I really liked her. She was superhot. I think I have a photo of me and her, sitting on my dad's custom chopper, which never actually started up. He was trying to build it from scratch.

Both Stan the Man and my dad were violent people. And they were tough. Vicious. Angry. Stupid. I imagine that back in the day they might have been the kind of guys who would go drinking and

Me in the Macalister River.

looking for trouble, and, if you took the bait from either of them, it would be a massive mistake.

My dad had another good friend named Jeff. He was a Czechoslovakian dude who had escaped from jail in his native land. I remember he had a tattoo he'd gotten in jail. It was this really bad drawing of a woman. Jeff decided he didn't like it, so he took it off with acid and sandpaper. It was kind of still half there. Only now it looked like he had also gotten shot where the tattoo was.

One all-time highlight from when I was young was heading off into the bush with my dad and Jeff and four or five of their mates. I was eleven or twelve by then. This was when Faberge's jeans came out. I had these skintight stretchy ones on. Jeff was a big hunter, so we went to New South Wales to go pig hunting for a week. I had a sawed-off shotgun with a sawed-off handle and a sawed-off nozzle. It was way shorter than usual so that I could hold it up. My dad made it for me so that I had something I could shoot, although I think he also made it because it was an incredibly illegal assault weapon. I think he thought that was funny.

We've built a fire, and we're starting to settle in when we feel this rumble in the ground. Jeff looks and me and says, "Get up in the fucking tree." So I grab my gun, and I get up in the tree, and then sure enough a pack of wild boars come flying in, straight through the fire. Maybe twenty of them. Running. I can't say I was scared. I was just thinking about how cool it was to see them up close, and how cool it was going to be to kill them.

We dropped out of the tree, and there was one of them lagging behind. I shot it. To my surprise, it went down. But then it got up and started running, straight back at me. I don't think it was trying to come after me. I just think it got rocked from the bullet and wanted to run away. I just happened to be right in the direction it headed.

I needed to reload. I was really nervous about getting more bullets into the gun. Even though there were adults around me who had weapons, too, apparently this was my shot. I'd like to say that if it had gotten really close to me, someone would have shot it for me, but Jeff was standing right next to me, and I don't remember him pulling a gun.

I shot the pig. Over and over again, until it fell on the ground.

I shot it in the face, and in the eye, and watched the bullet come straight out of the back of its head. Shot its brains out. And this thing was still squealing and carrying on. The pig dog came over, and the boar's tusk went into the dog's collar. The boar flicked him, and the dog went flying. This was a big dog. I think it was a pit bull. It had a leather collar with studs on it, and the thing snapped right off. And then the pig died.

The guys hooked it up to a tree, and Jeff told me to hit it with a meat cleaver, right in the dick, and then chop down into its rib cage. I had to stick my arms inside and pull out the intestines and organs. I think everyone was getting off on watching a kid do this. I impaled an animal that was way bigger than I was, and then chopped its head off. I spent like half an hour with this meat cleaver, just trying to chop through the bone and get that head off. Blood splattering everywhere. Everyone was really proud of me. I was really proud of myself. I took the head off, and then I put it on my head, posing like that with the gun, for a photo. That's probably the thing my father's friends always remembered about me. They'd bring it up for years afterward, when they were drunk and hanging out at the house. I remember I ate its kidneys. Jeff cooked them into a sort of meaty Jell-O blob, on a hot plate over a fire. "Bit o' garlic salt on there. It's good for ya, mate," they said. I thought they tasted good.

It was one of the greater weeks of my life. My brother Lee wasn't there, so I felt like it was my chance to hang with Dad and his friends. You know how, when you're little, you sense that your parents have an adult life when you're not around? That was one of those times when I got included in all that. My brothers got to know my dad better as they got older. But I didn't. My dad died so early. And I was in America so much. That was my quality time with him.

That was far from my only experience with firearms and wild beasts at a young age. I did a lot of rabbit hunting. One time I shot a kangaroo with a Bruno 270 rifle. I got weird about hunting later on, and violence in general. But when I was really young, I blindly went along with everything my dad and his friends did. I wanted to be like them. I didn't question the things I saw and the effect they had on me. I only did later on, as I got away from it all, and out on my own a little bit. When I had other influences in my life. Eventually, I got to know skateboard icons—Chris Miller, Lance Mountain—people I respected fully, who had never even touched a gun or gotten in a fistfight. So I saw there was another way. More and more I went soft on hurting people and killing animals. Now I'm a vegan. A couple of years ago, I even got an award from PETA. But back then? Fuck, yeah. Loved it.

A little while after the boar hunting trip, me and a friend took spearguns and went looking for trouble in the ocean, off the beach in Sandringham, where my dad and Marn lived. I was there with my father's speargun. Naturally my father had one of the highest-caliber spearguns on the face of the planet. My friend had a lesser weapon. I swam out with some goggles and a snorkel and flippers. We got out there pretty far.

I'm out there swimming around, minding my own business. Well, okay, I was out there looking for stuff to kill. But I look down, and about twenty-five feet beneath me, through murky water, I see a humongous stingray. Probably about the size of a small human. I took aim, shot him, and then *BOOM*—off he goes.

If you don't know, a speargun has a rope that attaches the spear to the gun. So this stingray takes off, to get away, but when the slack goes out of the rope, he doubles back, and heads directly at me, swimming upside down, at a ferocious speed. There was nothing I could do but take the hit, and so that's what I did. Right in the chest. I certainly would not have been the first person to die from having a stingray stab me, although I didn't know that at the time.

I thought I'd been stung. I looked around, but there were no stingers anywhere. I pulled my head above the surface to take a breath, and once again I felt the rope tighten. It occurred to me to let the gun go, but it had cost my dad three hundred dollars and I hadn't gotten permission to take it, so, out of fear of getting grounded, I held on. Sure enough, the stingray headed for me again.

I took a deep breath and tried to duck under it. It worked—I felt it swoop past me, then I came back up to the surface to yell to my friend. "This fucking thing is trying to kill me!" I told him to shoot it. He took aim. The only problem was, since the stingray was attacking me, if my friend missed, he would probably clip me instead.

So I started swimming. Meanwhile, my buddy fires, and hits it. "Swim away!" I yell, and the two of us head in opposite directions. We swam in all the way, with this frantic beast trapped between our two spearguns.

We dragged it onto the beach and pulled the spears out of it. A bunch of little stingray babies came out. I had killed a mommy. There were half a dozen of them. I felt like such a murderer. A baby killer. I grabbed all the babies in their little egg sacs, swam them back into the ocean one by one, and apologized to each of them for killing their mother. I would love to tell you they all miraculously survived, but in reality, they probably lived long enough to go into a fish's mouth.

As you can see, by this point, killing stuff already made me a little bit uncomfortable. I know the way I feel about violence has everything to do with my dad. Ever since I was little, I witnessed any number of brutal fistfights, which he made no attempt to hide from me.

One of them started at the counter of Ellistronics. This guy was arguing with my dad. Who knows what for. My dad was actually trying to be polite, for once. "If you don't like it, you can leave," he said. The guy reached over the counter and punched my dad in the face, and my father still didn't take the bait. He escorted the customer to the front door. The guy punched my dad again, and finally, in retaliation, my father punched the dude, with keys in his hand. A bunch of teeth popped right out of the guy's face, onto the floor.

I never saw my dad lose a fight, except for one time, years later. I was with my friend Chris Wright. We were in the alleyway on the side of Ellistronics, where my dad parked, and a guy came flying by and almost hit my father's car. Dad yelled after him, and the dude just stopped driving, stuck a giant arm out his car window, and pointed to the ground. Just like that, it was on.

The dude got out of the car and he was huge—maybe six foot four. Way bigger than my dad. I couldn't believe my father was still walking straight toward him. I was holding my dad back, but when they got into fighting range, I just stepped out of the way. Dad started throwing wild punches. He got the guy to move back a bit. Maybe he landed a couple. Then the guy kicked my dad in the chest, and Dad went flying back into the wall, before regaining his composure and getting back into a fighting stance. I had never seen that before. The guy had landed one on my father. Until that moment, I thought he was invincible.

So I jumped in. The guy was so tall, I literally leaped into the air and grabbed his head. I had him in a headlock, and he wasn't really even trying to fight me, until I started trying to smash his head into his own car door.

"All right! All right!" he said. "I'll fucking stop." I was unhinged. "Get in your fucking car!" I yelled. He drove off.

I looked at my dad.

"Fuck, you took your time jumping in," he said.

I asked him if I could get a ride home. He said no. He drove off in his Range Rover to do God knows what—I can now safely guess, whatever he was up to, he was *not* heading straight home to Marn.

That was the only time that happened. Usually, when my dad punched someone, it was over really quickly. Back when I was still a kid, we were going out on my dad's boat. My father wasn't a real boating kind of guy, but at one point he had this speedboat. It had a cool paint job. Black in the front, fading into gray, and then white in the back. He had been doing 90 kilometers per hour, no problem, but he was hell-bent on cracking 100. So he got a bigger blade, and 100 was his mission of the moment.

It was the two of us with these two girls—a friend of the family (actually my dad's friend's younger sister) and one of her friends. Now that I think about it, I didn't usually see this chick without her brother, my dad's friend, around, so who knows what was going on there. Anyway, another guy was there on the dock, getting his own boat ready, and he started talking to us a little. The guy was cussing, and my dad told him not to talk like that in front of ladies. "Go fuck yourself," the guy said. So my dad grabbed him by the shirt and punched him in the face. In those days, in Australia, sometimes it really could be go time, just like that.

Same as with the customer my dad fought at Ellistronics, a bunch of teeth immediately popped out. This guy's face was pretty bloodied up afterward, too. And even worse, his nose and stuff got shifted around. Instantly.

Just a few quick punches from my dad. And all of a sudden, this poor son of a bitch looked like a completely different person.

3.

SKATEBOARDING

IS AWESOME

Technically, skateboarding started for me when I was about six. Before skateboarding, I used to play a little footie. I was on a team. BMX, too.

I had a fake "aunt" and "uncle"—my mum's friends—who had a son, and one time I found his skateboard in their garage. Now, at this point, at least in my world in Australia, there was no professional skateboarding. This thing I found in the garage was plastic. A toy. It might as well have been a yo-yo. Little did I know thousands of other kids were making the same discovery I was, and this shitty little toy would be the reason I would leave Australia, travel the world, and be where I am now, knocking on the door of global domination.

At Sandy Tech, there were these twin brothers—Harry and Francis—that were into skateboards. In wood shop, I got a piece of chipboard, cut it into the shape of a skateboard, and then nailed it on some roller skates. It wouldn't even roll, because the wheels were so old. But I still stood outside of my mum's house all day on that thing, trying to do 360s. That was all it took. I was all in.

That monstrosity clearly wasn't going to get the job done, so I convinced my mum to get me a proper skateboard from the sports store. She wanted me to come around more often. I think she wanted to compete with my father for my time. But there was nothing to do once I got to her house. So I hounded her until she bought me a Variflex Headhunter. It was right when fat skateboards had just come out. I got the fattest board you could get, and fat wheels, and fat trucks. A lot of my early skating happened around her house.

Skateboarding grabbed me right away.

Instantly.

As soon as I got that board, I went to the Parkdale Bowl and rolled in. Not standing, mind you. No way. This was a legitimate ten-foot-deep keyhole bowl. And it was *fucked*. I mean, this was Australia. They don't know what the fuck they're doing. It was this rickety, dangerous death trap. If I came across it now, there is zero chance I would go near this thing. Nonetheless, I rolled in, on my ass, and then, in the bottom, got up and started rolling, back and forth.

I was by myself a lot when I was a kid. Wandering around by myself. Hiding out in that alley when I skipped school. I think skateboarding was something that finally made me feel content to be alone. It just made sense to me. I didn't need any other equipment. Or any other people. Just me and my skateboard. That's it. Plus, skating helped me get out of my head. When you're skating, it's hard to worry about anything else, other than the next trick.

The Beaumaris ramp was the first vert ramp I ever saw. Fifteen, twenty minutes from my house. That was the first half-pipe. I'm a vert skater. A ramp skater. I was hooked. All I cared about was that ramp. All day. Every day. Learning how to drop in. That was the first place I saw people who were good, instead of just kids dicking around.

A guy called Chris Payne was my first skateboard idol. He had punk rock spiky hair. He made me want to be a rock star. He would drop in and do little airs. And Rock and Rolls, which is when you put your board up on the deck, and then turn it back in. He would smash his board into the deck. Really aggressively put it up there. That was so impressive to me. I would try to show off in front of him, as best I could.

I localized the Beaumaris ramp. It became my territory, like a surfer owning his local wave. I learned to skate on that ramp. I

I'm about fourteen here, localizing the Beaumaris ramp.

became good there. I became the person that went there the most. I put my time in. And the better you become, the more you come to own that ramp. It wasn't like I went around being a dick to everybody, but if someone was causing problems and needed to leave, I was the guy that would tell you—and you'd have to listen to me. I localized every one of my local ramps. Beaumaris. Prahran. My mum's house wasn't home. Dad and Marn's house wasn't either. The ramps were.

There was Mordialloc ramp, a big fucking black steel ramp. On hot days, you could fry an egg on it. Literally. We would do it, for a joke, and just watch them sizzle. I remember, if you fell on the ramp, you'd have to lean on your pads to get up. You couldn't touch it with bare skin, or it would burn the fuck out of you. Ah, Mordy, mate! Mordy was the first wide ramp, with bigger transitions. (The transition is the curved part of the ramp, where the flat transitions into the walls, and vice versa.) Beauie was so little by comparison. The transition was similar to a backyard pool. I think it was maybe ten feet wide. But Mordy had a channel—like a roll-in in the middle—that was around thirty feet wide.

Skateboarding was the first time in my life I had a bunch of friends. Right off the bat. Really good ones, too. It was still a kind of unusual thing to be a skater back then. At some point, every kid tries to ride a skateboard, because it's affordable. Everyone can get their hands on a board. And it looks cool. But it's hard, and most kids give up after a week.

Those of us who didn't give up had a lot in common. It was like a code we shared. To be a skater, you were probably a pretty competitive person. You had to have spent a *lot* of time by yourself, working on it. And you probably had some respect for yourself—a bit of an attitude—because you had managed to get good at something that you took really seriously.

Before long, skateboarding became my whole world. At dinner, I would make little skate ramps out of mashed potatoes and visualize tricks on them. I did that every night with all my food, but we ate a lot of mashed potatoes with my stepmum, so that was the go-to.

Finding out about skateboarding in America—*real* skateboarding—wasn't easy back then. There was no Internet. There weren't even any skateboard stores. Max Water Ski World was the shop in my area that stocked all the skate gear. That should tell you something. And the skateboards were there before the magazines. Before the videos. My first really good skateboard was a Lance Mountain board with aborigines on the graphic, running and skating. It was my first American board. It cost $300 to get it set up, even back in the 1980s. I treated it like it was a Ferrari. I don't remember where the money came from, but I never saved anything. I probably convinced somebody to buy it for me.

The first skate magazine that I saw was *Thrasher,* with Tony Hawk on the cover doing a Smith grind. It was all tie-dyed different colors. And he had pink on: a pink helmet and a pink shirt. I remember thinking, *Tony Hawk. Fuck, there he is!* Before that, Tony Hawk and the other pro skaters were just these mythical beings that the guy behind the counter would talk about when we came into the shop. We just heard rumors about them and the tricks they were pulling off. "Did you hear that this dude Tony Hawk did a Fingerflip?" I specifically remember calling some dude in a skate shop a moron and telling him that was physically impossible. And then there was Tony Hawk, on the cover of another *Thrasher* magazine, doing an Airwalk.

The first video I saw was *Future Primitive,* with Lance Mountain and Tony Hawk. They sold it at Max Water Ski World. A skater friend bought it, and I saw it over at his house. The *Bones Brigade* video was made before that, but we got that after in Australia. Tony was still a little bony kid in *Future Primitive*. He did a 720 at the end of his video part. In Australia, there were maybe a couple of dudes that could do a 180. A 180 is a half turn on your board, in the air. A 720 is two full rotations. Like a lot of things Tony Hawk could do on a skateboard, that didn't seem humanly possible. But there it was, on the video.

Seeing the hard evidence that these tricks could actually be done was life-changing stuff: After I saw Tony Hawk do an Airwalk in a photograph, I was pretty sure I was gonna be a pro. After I saw *Future Primitive*, I was absolutely fucking positive.

I wasn't the only one. The *Bones Brigade* videos are what made skating catch on in Australia. The government built all the skateparks. I don't think there's a single private skatepark in Australia—even now they're all public. Still to this day there are massive concrete parks, and you don't have to pay any money to skate them. Because nobody sues anybody there.

Harry and Francis—the twin brothers who were my best friends when I started skating—moved away, up to Queensland. That meant I was the only skater in my school. This would be the era where I began to routinely have the shit beaten out of me. I hated it, as you might imagine. And I hated how the guys that beat me up would tell me they were going to do it beforehand. For the longest time, that was the stress of my life.

My fear of violence grew as I got older. I'm a nutcase on a skateboard, and then throw in the whole "tattooed Australian" thing, and people have always figured that "this guy *must* be a maniac." But I didn't want to fight. I never did. Although I didn't want anyone to know that. "Punch the one that hits you first." That was my dad's advice. "Do not listen to your father." That was the advice from Marn, the antiviolence person in the house. I know my stepmum thought I was a violent person. If you'd ask her, she'd say there was a streak of violence running through my childhood. Maybe I *did* get in fights sometimes, but fuck, it was self-defense. People were beating *me* up. I definitely never enjoyed it.

The worst violence I ever perpetrated in my life was directed at myself, on a skateboard. My first major injury—the first of many—was when I broke my arm in Queensland. I caught a bus up there and stayed with Harry and Francis for two weeks. Skating the whole time. It was a twenty-four-hour bus ride. I have a hard time sitting still now. But in my early teens? My God—that was the worst day of my life.

The day I was about to leave, I was skating in a bowl. My board locked up, and I went to fall, but then the board shot me into one of the concrete walls. I was gonna hit my head, so I stuck my arm out. I fractured my wrist, which is bad. (Warning: this is about to get a bit gruesome.) Even worse, the forearm bone shot out of the back of my elbow (which dislocated my elbow, naturally) and fractured a bone in the top half of my arm, too. The biggest crash of my life, at least back then. I passed out on the spot when I saw a gaping hole in my arm. Then they took me to the hospital.

I couldn't use my arm for six months. It wouldn't straighten. But I was so obsessed with skating that it didn't slow me down. In a roundabout way, it actually helped me get better. I was just getting good enough to do airs, but I had a cast on for six months. Without getting too technical, the first air anybody ever learns is a Backside air. The Backside air is the easiest one to do. Everyone's high air is a Backside air. But right when it was my time to learn airs, I only had one arm. So I learned Indie airs first, which are way harder. I would roll in, pump the wall, grab my board down on the flat, and then just *yank*, and do this air. That was my trick for the longest time. So the day my arm finally straightened, and I could do a Backside air, my Backside air was way better and higher than the group's, because I had put in all this hard time skating with one arm.

By my teens, skateboarding had evolved way beyond the plastic toy phase, even where we were in Australia. There were tons of us doing it. Compared to a lot of my friends, I knew I was good. Still, there were maybe fifteen, twenty dudes ahead of me in Melbourne alone. But one day—with a little bit of a kick in the ass—I found out I was *really* good.

I was on the ramp, doing Frontside Ollies. That's more technical skate talk—basically, you roll up to the top of the ramp, make a quick 180 to the left while airborne, then land and roll back down, no hands. That was kind of a big deal at that point. And the thing is, I did them easy. And that day, another skater, Gary Valentine, was there. Gary was my age, but he'd already been to America. They even wrote an article about him in a skate magazine. "Fifteen and Filthy," it was called. I knew him from being around at the Mordialloc ramp. Gary was watching me do Frontside Ollies, and he was like, "Go big. Pose it. Why not?" I made a little tweak in my approach, and I did what he said. I went HUGE.

No one in Australia was doing that at the time. Maybe three people in the whole world were.

Holy shit.

Then, with Gary pushing me on, I kept going, and just reeled off some next-level maneuvers.

Bang, I got up off the ramp, chest-high.

Bang—Tail Grab. First person in Australia to ever do a Tail Grab.

Bang—Stalefish. First person in Australia to ever do a Stalefish. (That's when you grab your board behind your leg and . . . ah, you don't give a shit. But if you know what I'm talking about, you know what I'm talking about.)

All this happened in a grand total of twenty minutes. I guess I had been working up to all this without even realizing it. By the end of that day, I had my first sponsor—Osmosis Surf Shop.

I don't know why I got better than other people. I had friends who were sponsored before me. It could just have been my love for the game, I guess. I mean, those guys loved it, too. But those guys had a choice. Maybe it was like what you hear about basketball players coming from these gangster-ass situations and developing the mentality that sports are the only way out. Some of the guys I knew were smart. They were gonna get a job somewhere. In the back of their minds, the attitude was probably, *A career in skateboarding? Let's be serious.* But the future looked pretty bleak from where I was standing, so I figured I might as well live it up while I could. My thought was, *Hey, if I can pull this off, at least I'll get a couple years out of it.* I was always that guy. Live it up. Because it's all going to end, any day now.

You have to understand, skateboarding was the *only* thing that I cared about. Imagine getting good at the only thing you care about. I am not exaggerating. Nothing else mattered, at all. I've never loved anything like I loved skateboarding. All I ever wanted to do was fly around on my skateboard, enjoying myself, and I figured it out, in a way that was so gratifying. Every day on the ramp, I would be literally coming in my pants with enjoyment. It was *perfect.* And that brought confidence.

Two guys who need to get mentioned here are Gregor Rankin and Lee Ralph. Gregor and Lee were the first two really good skateboarders in Australia—although they came from New Zealand. The first time I saw them was at a contest. By this time, I was sponsored by Peninsula Surf Center, and Peninsula had a ramp in the back. By "sponsored," I mean I was basically this little rookie rat-dude who got discounts on grip tape. In the scheme of things, I was still a beginner. These guys were next level.

Most of the time, a contest like this would have been just the usual local nobodies, like me. But the talk beforehand was about these two dudes who had already competed in America. Lee and Gregor broke into a car the night before the contest, and then slept in it. Lee's got sneakers with fucking holes in them. They were barely on his feet. And he's a massive dude—bigger than me. Probably one of the biggest skateboarders ever. With a beard and shit. We were like, "Who the fuck is this guy?" And he proceeded to annihilate the ramp like I had never seen anybody do in the flesh. And then Gregor did, as well.

They didn't even have a skateboard. They borrowed one at the contest. Some piece of shit skateboard, and someone else's kneepads. People were just dumbfounded. It was a jaw-dropping exhibition. Before too long, they became the lords of skateboarding. They owned Australia. They found unknown skaters with some talent, and then they built them into pros. They built Ben and Tas Pappas, two other pro skaters who later came to America. And they built me. I was the first one. Not too long after Gregor and Lee got to Australia, Gary Valentine got them to watch me, and then, about three tricks later, I was in. It was this elite group. The only one that mattered in Australian skateboarding.

I take pieces of people, things I see in them that I can use to make myself better on my way. People I look up to. Gregor is definitely in that category. He was a version of what I wanted to be. A model. A guy from Australia (or New Zealand—whatever) going to America to be successful in skateboarding. He had won an amateur competition at Mount Trashmore, a legendary contest. To hear Gregor tell it, he went into a zone. Blacked out. Couldn't hear the crowd at all. He just felt himself destroying the world, with every wall, every trick, and every adjustment he made along the way. I made him tell me this story many, many times. And I figured that in order to get to America like he had, I had to imitate the things he did as much as possible.

Gregor was a hard-ass and one of the most intense people I have ever met. Total commitment. Total discipline. He didn't drink. He didn't smoke. He'd never had sex. He was like twenty-six at the time—a full decade older than me. He tried to pass off the whole no-sex thing as this super-hard-core decision he had made. In reality, it might have just been that he wasn't confident enough to talk to girls. But he was intelligent enough to convince you that, whatever he was doing, that was exactly the way he intended to be, and that he wasn't just a loser.

Gregor is where my shit-talking came from. Gregor was, and is still to this day, the meanest person I have ever met in my life. I hate him for what he did to me back then. Him and Lee called me Goober. I think that was just the most insulting nickname they could come up with. That's what they were going for. They would get pissed off at me, out of nowhere. "Fuck off, Goober, ya stupid fucking cunt! Get the fuck off the ramp!" Like, a full-on adult, yelling at a kid. For no reason. I'm over it, now. But put it this way—if adult me was there, watching what he did to me as a kid, I would punch him in the face, no questions asked. I loved him. And he was such a dick.

Within six months of the first time I saw them, Gregor and Lee had a surf shop in Melbourne called Snake Pit. Again, there were no skate shops at this point. There was just surf people selling skate-boards in a little corner of the store. Hardcore Enterprises, the distributors of all skateboards in Australia, financially backed Snake Pit.

Snake Pit was the first place I saw Tony Hawk in person. Through Hardcore, Gregor had paid for the Bones Brigade skaters to make an appearance in Australia. They were there to skate some demos and to take part in the biggest contest we'd ever had—the Ramp Riot. I was pretty amped to meet some of these skateboarding gods in person, so I made sure to know when they were coming in.

I was waiting for them in the shop. And then there they were.

There's Mike McGill. He's a shit skater. The worst style ever. So I didn't care about him. But still, it was impressive that he was here, in my little skate shop.

Then in walked Lance Mountain, Steve Caballero, and Tony Hawk. They were looking around the store, at clothes and stuff. I felt utter disgust for the three other people in the store, all of whom were pretending to be skateboarders, holding skateboards, none of whom knew who the fuck was standing right next to them.

I was awestruck. It was such a big deal to me. Nothing's ever been a bigger deal to me than those people. I looked at them like they were gods. Tony Hawk, to me, was bigger than Elvis.

I got to meet Lance Mountain a little while after this, when he made another trip to Australia for the next Ramp Riot. He knew Gregor and Lee. Those guys didn't make it huge in America, but they were legit. Top ten in the world vert skateboarders—and at that point in time, vert skateboarding was all that skateboarding was. Gregor and Lee picked me up. They were my ride to the contest, two hours away, in Bells Beach. And Lance was sitting in the fucking car. Lance is the main skater in the whole *Future Primitive* video. At that point, he's maybe not the best skateboarder, but he's top five, for sure, plus he's the funniest and most outgoing. I could relate to that—being a little more creative than just your standard, stock skater dude. It was a two-hour drive, and it was a struggle to maintain my composure the entire time. Not once did I even look in Lance's direction.

My father had paid for me to enter this Ramp Riot. I was sixteen by then. My parents only went to maybe two skate competitions ever, but that was one of them. Tony Hawk was there. That's when I met Sergie Ventura, too, another pro skater I know to this day.

I was freaking out. It was a contest with really famous pros—like twenty of them. I was in the fourth heat with a bunch of Tony Alva's dudes—Jeff Grosso, Craig Johnson—people I had seen in videos and magazines. I didn't even have the balls to drop in to practice. Someone had to tell me it was okay. "Have a ride, dude. Drop in." "Oh. All right. Thank you!" I dropped in, did a couple tricks, and got out, shitting myself.

I got sixteenth—the second-highest-placed Australian. This was no small thing. I had the ride of my life. I didn't even exist at that point, but as far as I was concerned, that needed to be the ride that would be my ticket out of there. It always was. At every contest, on every scale, I always thought: *This is the one that will get me out of here.* The one that would show everybody that I could do it.

I have video of that ride. For how good I was at that time, I really did nail it. I stalled a hand plant, which was a risky thing to do back then. By stalling over the deck, you're balancing your whole body on one hand, and falling off becomes a huge possibility. But I didn't.

On the way back, when Gregor and Lee dropped me off, Lance Mountain spoke to me for the first time all day. "You skated really good," he said. Holy shit. Lance Mountain just paid me a compliment!

Fuck, Lance Mountain says hello to me *now*, to this *day*, and I *still* think it's cool.

I got out of the car, stoked out of my balls.

4.

GETTING THE FUCK
OUT OF AUSTRALIA

The day I turned sixteen, I was legal to leave school. So that's what I did. By then, my passion for skateboarding had kicked in royally and I was getting pretty good. So I made my mother and my father meet me at a pub, and I told them I really needed to work on my skating. Support me for six months, I said, and then I'll go to America and become a pro. After they finished laughing at me, they informed me that I was an idiot. Skateboarding wasn't even a real sport, they said. But I begged.

See? They really did love me. This was a ridiculous story. Back then, skateboarding *wasn't* real. No one knew who Tony Hawk was. The X Games didn't exist. No one had a *job* riding a skateboard, at least as far as my parents were concerned. Truthfully, I didn't even know how being a pro worked, myself. But all I wanted to do was skate.

My parents hated each other, but I made them get together so I could pitch my master plan. I was like, "Look, I can't dillydally. I need to skate every day. I'm gonna move to America, I'm gonna turn pro, and then you won't have to pay for me to live. But the catch is, for the next six months, I'm gonna need you to feed me and to not make me get a job, because I'm gonna need to train." They both agreed. Probably because they'd never seen me motivated to do *anything* before.

Gary Valentine, the prodigy, was the number one vert skater in Australia. We were best friends at the time. He'd already been to America, so he knew some people. He was going again, and I wanted to go with him. Gregor said it was too soon for me, but I didn't give a shit. I mean, as I've mentioned, Gregor was kind of a cunt. Gary knew Lance Mountain, so supposedly we were going to stay at Lance's house. That was pretty trippy. And Gary said he could introduce me to some other people. Otherwise, there wasn't much of what you might call a plan. Just: Go to America, skate my ass off, and try to make shit happen.

No one was paying my way. I saved my money. My dad let me sell my dirt bike. Once again, this was a very crazy thing for him to go along with. I'm sure part of him was just thinking, *Thank God. See you later.* But the other part of it had to be some actual respect for my dream. I can only imagine how passionate I must have been during that pitch I gave him at the pub.

My parents did support me for a couple months, but then they told me to get a fucking job. I did some time at Ellistronics. My dad was a really bad boss. He was a cocksucker to me, to prove a point to all the other employees. Everyone that worked there was a computer pussy, and I couldn't have been less interested in all that stuff. My father knew even less than I did. If I ever asked my dad a question, he was like, "I don't fucking know. Why don't you ask one of the other guys?"

Technically, Ellistronics was always there as a fallback for me, but all of us knew that wasn't really going to work out. I think my dad assumed that I would end up on welfare, with him supporting me. There was definitely a strong possibility of a very bleak adulthood for me. That's the feeling I got from everybody, anyway.

I had other jobs, trying to save up to get to America. I picked apples in the country somewhere. For about a week, anyway. I thought that was really cool, for some reason. I was a courier. I was a bricklayer—a brickie's laborer, we call it in Australia. I worked in a supermarket, Safeway. When I had that job, I lived with my mother in Rosebud, this town which is a town in the middle of bullshit whoop-whoop nowhere. My mum had gotten married again, and she moved to Rosebud with her husband, who was a millionaire. He had been a water skier. He was in the *Guinness Book of World Records* for skiing all the way from Victoria to Tasmania. By this time he was big and fat, but he was the nicest guy ever. He sold building supplies—bricks, rocks, wood, and stuff like that—and he was working all the time, so I barely ever saw him.

I was a trolley boy at Safeway, bringing the shopping carts in from the lot. I had a uniform that made me look like a massive, gigantic douche: gray leather shoes, zipped up on both sides; gray plaid pants; a white button-down shirt; and a black leather tie. In those days it was actually not uncommon for Aussie trolley boys to wear that kind of getup.

My flowing locks were just long enough that I had to slick them behind my ears to keep them out of my face and properly represent the trolley boy profession. This look was apparently so enticing that one time this old chick tried to ask me if I wanted to go back to her house, after I put her groceries in her car. Straight up propositioned me. But I was so nervous, I pulled out of it before I even realized what she was asking me.

Looking back, it's kind of surprising I could miss something like that. Along with all the drinking, and the drugs, and people punching each other, sex had been all around me, in my face, ever since I was young. By the time my mum tried telling me about the birds and the bees, when I was about ten, it was already way too late. There were naked people around Mum's house all the time. People had already been fucking around me.

I think my mum thought that if my dad had all the guns and toys and guy stuff at his place, she could compete by making her house a place where I could do whatever I wanted. I think that was her angle. If I wanted to smoke a cigarette in front of her, fine. If I could get laid, have at it. My mum personally showed me naked photos of this really hot friend she had. Her name was Kim. These pictures blew my horny little mind. They were not artistic photos. They were straight-up spread-eagle. "Kim's a bit of a whore," my mother informed me, on more than one occasion. I would hear stories. You know—Kim had sex with so-and-so. Or, this or that guy came over the other night. So early on I started putting two and two together. I remember wanting to fuck Kim for the longest time.

There were no rules for me when it came to sex. I had a thirteen-year-old girlfriend when I was eleven. She lived in a house near my mum. That's how I met her. And she was allowed to stay the night, in a room, alone, with me. She had hair on her vagina, and my penis was still completely bald.

My mum would talk about this girlfriend in a weird, suggestive way. To let me know she knew everything that was going on, and that it was okay by her. I use the word *girlfriend* very loosely. I don't remember having a single conversation with this chick. I just had an urge to put my penis in someone, and she thought I was cute. She was crazy. I mean—if you're a thirteen-year-old girl, why would you have sex with an eleven-year-old? There was always drama. It was almost like a weird little love triangle—eleven-year-old me, my crazy thirteen-year-old girlfriend, and my mother. The girl would tell my mum stuff, and it would come back to me, and I would just be baffled by the whole situation. I mean, really? Don't look at me—I'm fucking *eleven*!

If I missed my cue from the old lady in the supermarket parking lot, I didn't make the same mistake with another older woman. She was ten years older than me—twenty-six, when I was sixteen. She worked at Snake Pit, and she looked like Marilyn Monroe, with bleach blond curly hair. Very pasty. Big ass. Superhot. I asked her to go to dinner with me one night and she thought that was adorable. I had that spark of cockiness already. She cooked for me, and then after dinner we hung out at her house. Man, if I could go back in time and be a fly on the wall for that evening of seduction. I mean, she was an adult woman who looked like Marilyn Monroe . . . and I was a sixteen-year-old kid from Sandringham. I had holes in the sleeves of my long-sleeve T-shirt that I could stick my thumbs through.

She showed me photos of her from when she was a kid. She was very obsessed with her youth, I think, and trying to get that back. That's where I came in, I guess. After the photo albums, she jumped on me. None of what went down that night was my decision. She was totally in the driver's seat. Everything she did blew my mind more than the thing that she did before it. *Wow, you're taking your top off? And now you're undoing my fly?* I came several times, in rapid succession, and just pretended it hadn't happened. She completely knew every time, of course, though I thought I was pulling it off at the time. She put me to bed, and then woke me up and gave me some toast, and off I went, on my way. I remember walking down the street thinking, *No one is gonna fucking believe this.*

My old man thought she was the hottest chick he'd ever seen, so I couldn't wait to tell him. "You slept with that? You are fucking shitting me," he said. I told him right away. Fuck, yeah. The only way he could have been more proud is if somehow I could have lined it up so he *also* could fuck her.

While I was still biding my time, waiting to go to America with Gary Valentine on my six-month tourist visa, I spent New Year's Eve on a houseboat in the Murray River, with my dad and Marn, plus Roger and Misty, a married couple who were close friends of my dad's.

I was not very happy that night. I didn't want to be there. I was sixteen. I had the Metallica *Master of Puppets* cassette, and the whole time I was pumping it into my head with a Walkman. Almost like my form of a sulking protest. Metallica were—and still are—a massive influence on my life. At nighttime around that time, I would drink and listen to them, and I used to write lyrics all over my skateboard. There would be all these little hidden things, in marker. *"I rule the midnight air. The destroyer."* I'd be listening to Metallica, wasted, and I would feel so fucking motivated. The songs would make me think of a million tricks to do the next day. I could dream so big. And it actually *would* carry over to the next day. I'd wake up hungover, but still focused and not scared to take risks on the ramp, or even die. I would do anything on a skateboard. I wasn't scared of pain. I had this anger in me, like a lot of teenagers. But Metallica helped me point that anger in the right direction.

So this New Year's Eve, on the houseboat, I spent a lot of the night sitting alone reading the lyrics from the little *Master of Puppets* cassette booklet. I had connected with the music so much that, for the first time, I was motivated enough to want to know what the fuck they were saying. I read it all the way through. Over and over again. Until I could figure out what all the words were, and what they meant. Thinking, *Wow, maybe reading could be handy one day.* For the longest time afterward, if people would ask me what books I had read, I would say, *"Master of Puppets."* The lyrics were the first thing I ever read. I feel like Metallica made me think that I might not want to be a dyslexic fucking idiot my whole life.

When it got close to midnight that night, my dad and his friends got me to take my headphones off, and we all went to some pub off the side of the river. They were celebrating the New Year. I was the only kid there.

Everyone's counting down, then the clock strikes twelve, and people are cheering. And then, I look over, and . . . Roger's *making out* with Marn.

My father's friend, and my stepmum.

Holy shit! This is a situation.

But then, I look over to the other side of the table . . . and *Dad's* making out with *Misty.*

I tried to hide. My hand was over my face, and my hair was over my hand. I'm leaning down into the tabletop, in shock and disbelief. Trying to not be there. But then someone lifted my head up and started making out with me.

Misty.

I was sixteen, and these drunk people are making out with each other in some sort of free-for-all. And this crazy bitch just made out with me, in front of her husband, who I've known my whole life. I tensed up, waiting for Roger to come over and flatten me. But he didn't. Nobody did anything. And I know they all saw it. It went on for like two minutes.

Nobody ever said anything about it, either. That mind-boggling situation happened, and then the next day it was just . . . over. Maybe I don't remember. Maybe I was really sketched out the next day, and I've forgotten. But no one said anything to me, and Dad and Marn went about their business. I don't recall spending weeks afterward thinking about how I had just watched all these adults in a group make-out session. Or about the fact that I had been roped into it. I just moved on.

Not long after that, I was at a party at my dad's house and Misty was there. And so was her sister, Tracie, a redhead. Tracie was the crazy one. I'm sitting on the couch, watching a movie. It was late and the party had died down. Dad's gone to sleep, and it's just the three of us. To think—the innocence of it all. I'm on a couch with both of them, at two in the morning, and I didn't even see it coming. Tracie started rubbing my leg. She's married, too. I've known her husband, Alan, my whole life.

This is crazy. I get up and go to the bathroom. And then Misty follows me in. She starts making out with me. Attacks me. Doesn't say a word as she takes me into the spare room. I remember not lasting too long. And then sneaking back into my room, and sleeping, not believing what had just happened.

Dad told me later on that he knew. I called bullshit. "Look," he said, "I went into your bedroom that night, and you weren't there, and then I heard you fucking her in the other room." And still, it wasn't a big deal. He was just letting me know that he knew.

How could he be cool with that? Me and his friend's wife! But at the time, again, I don't remember thinking that much of it.

I guess they were all just fucking each other behind each other's back. Everyone. I saw naked photos of Misty a long time ago, while I was looking for a porno tape in my dad's stuff. (It was called *Naked Lunch,* although not to be confused with the movie where the guy gets high on insect repellant.) When I found the photo, I remember asking Marn, "Did you guys all sleep with each other, or something?" "Don't be silly," she said. "Your dad doesn't even like redheads."

Really? How could she not know? Dad liked anything with a pussy. I thought, *You really have no idea who you're married to.* I can't say for sure, but it wouldn't surprise me if *everyone* who was around back then fucked *everybody* else, at some point or another.

Around this time, right before I went to America, my mum sent me to this camp that a holistic doctor, a naturopath, recommended. My mum's a big tofu-eating hippie type of person, and she's always known crazy people like that. The naturopath told her I was depressed and that the camp would help me. I'm pretty gullible, so off I went. I think I was there for about a week. I was sixteen and I was way younger than everybody else. There were all these alcoholics, and people that had gone bankrupt. Fat ladies and old men. The woman that ran the place—also a naturopath—was married to the guy that sent me there.

They were trying to do meditation and hypnosis. Whatever that was supposed to do, it didn't work. Then one day we all had to go to this pool. So off we all went, and then the woman in charge—the doctor's wife—told everybody to take their clothes off and get in. I was one of the last people in the pool, because I did not want to get naked around all these people. When I finally did, I remember a couple of women there looking at my penis. It was creepy, having old ladies staring like that. But also kind of cool. Let's be honest.

The head lady told us to pair up. I froze. Everyone else picked a partner, and the only person left was this old man. That made it the oldest, most wrinkly guy in the class, along with the youngest dude. Everyone was supposed to cradle someone. I would say the old guy had to be seventy. And just like that he's cradling me like a baby. "Relax," the lady said. "It's just like being reborn." But all I could focus on was the old man whose naked penis was right next to my back. If the whole rebirthing thing ever happened, I must have missed it.

And then I had to do it to him. I cradled an old man, in a pool.

Just afterward, the naturopath lady cornered me in the water. I had no idea what she was talking about. I was more aware of her pubic hair brushing against my penis. I may have missed a few signals in those days, but I was definitely aware that she was hitting on me. At the end of it all, she volunteered to drive me back to my mum's house. That's when she pulled over and jumped on me.

A couple days later, my mum said the lady's husband wanted to talk to me. I hadn't told Mum about anything that had happened. I went to his office, and the guy got in my face and tried to intimidate me over me doing something with his wife. I was backed up against a corner. There was a big old-school phone on the table, and I threatened to hit him with it. I didn't know what else to do. This was the guy who had made me go to the camp in the first place.

I remember telling my mum afterward. The whole thing. There were no real repercussions to speak of. "We should get our money back," she said.

I couldn't wait to go to America.

PART TWO

5.

THE FIRST TIME I WENT TO AMERICA WAS AWESOME

The day I landed in America was the greatest day of my life.

I got off the plane at LAX. This would have been maybe the second or third time I'd flown anywhere. And never internationally before. I was seventeen. The door at the terminal opened, and I saw all the American cars and American people for the first time. They looked so different to me. You may not know this, Americans, but to us foreigners, you all look like you're on TV. I was so happy, so excited, to have finally made it to the land of skateboarding. *This is the place where Tony Hawk lives, and now I'm here, too.*

If you had been there, you would have seen it right on my face. It wasn't just about skating. I was free. I could do whatever I wanted. This was my ticket to be something. To not be a nobody. To not be a burden to my dad—a loser with dyslexia who is always getting beaten up, and getting into trouble that I didn't go looking for. I've never been more thrilled to be anywhere in my life.

There was no one there waiting to meet us. No one knew I was coming to the States at all. We were just two lone wolves, me and Gary Valentine. We had a place to land at Lance Mountain's house. But for one night, maybe. If we were lucky. We for sure weren't gonna stay there for six months.

You were supposed to have a thousand dollars for every month you were going to be in America, so technically I should have had six grand. I just lied when I got to Customs. I think I actually had fifty bucks. The only luggage I brought was an old hiking backpack. I packed a skateboard, my pads, a set of wheels, some shorts, and some T-shirts. I brought a sleeping bag, too, because I was going to sleep under ramps. And my parents knew that.

It wasn't that hard leaving Australia. Out of any family member, I was the least like an actual member of the family, from as far back as I can remember. I was just the odd guy out. Pool parties and barbecues, I'd just be standing back and looking around, thinking, *Who the fuck are these people?* So I became an American pretty much immediately.

Directly from LAX, me and Gary took a taxi. (He had a little bit more money than me. I'm sure he paid.) We went to this ramp, the H ramp, that Gary knew about from his previous trip to the States. It was the first miniramp with a spine and hips. What that means is, there were multiple miniramps back-to-back, so you could go over the first one and straight onto the next one, and then off the side of that one, and jump over to another one, and so on, all over the place.

Right off the bat, this was it. This was the America I had been working to get to. Dreaming of. Back in Australia, we had just gotten miniramps, period. Here, they'd laid out a whole course of them. Holy shit.

I was amped out of my face to be riding this monstrosity. And then Jinx showed up. (Marty Jimenez was his real name, but to everybody, he was just Jinx.) Jinx was kind of a shit pro, to be honest. When I look back, this dude was around for ten years, and he wasn't really good at anything. He was actually kind of an insult to the game. But still, to me? Then? Fuck—that's Jinx! In Australia, this is a guy you see in magazines and videos. Here, he actually shows up to skate. And I'm skating with him.

We ended up staying at Lance Mountain's house for about two weeks. By this point, Lance was married and had a kid. The fact that he was responsible and not a loser was pretty trippy. I'd never met any skaters that were full-on dads and husbands. We stuck around a bit longer than his wife probably would have liked. (A couple weeks after we left, Lance and his wife got some crank call, and to this day, I think they both believe it was me.)

Lance had a ramp in his backyard, which was pretty next level. I learned a bunch of tricks out there. I don't remember if Lance remembered me from that long car ride with Gregor and Lee in Australia. Either way, I'm sure I reminded him numerous times. I hounded him to the point of being annoying, just trying to pick up any wisdom I could. You could tell Lance was really committed to helping fellow skaters and furthering the sport and all that bullshit. "If you learn three tricks every day," he told me, "you'll definitely go pro." So that's what I started to do. Religiously.

Lance took a picture of me that went in *Transworld*. That made me the first Australian with a full-page photo in one of the magazines.

Skating was still such an American-only thing. I think Lance wanted to say that Gary and me were the first foreigners who might be able to do some damage. It was a very glamorous shot—I was all acne'd out, and I was totally in the zone, trying to land my trick, which, for the record, was a frontside 50-50 270 Revert Out.

Lance also took me to meet Stacy Peralta, one of the original Dogtown guys, and the guy who was responsible for Powell-Peralta, the company that put Lance and Tony Hawk in the Bones Brigade. Out of nowhere, Lance said that Stacy should put *me* in the Bones Brigade.

I couldn't comprehend what I was hearing—could this really be happening? Could it really be that easy?

The answer is no. Which wasn't a big shock or anything. I may think I'm awesome, but I'm not insane.

Then Stacy asked Lance if I could do any street skating, they both laughed a bit, and that was the end of that. I didn't get the joke at the time. A few years later, as you'll see, the joke made more sense to me—but by the time I got it, I wasn't laughing.

The first event I entered in California was a Vans amateur contest, somewhere around Los Angeles. It was another one of these big miniramp things, with all the extensions. There was a pair of twins there, Ben and Matthew Schroeder. They were huge. Way bigger than me. Older than me, too—maybe twenty-one? They both looked like He-Man, right down to the haircut. (Although I couldn't have looked too different—later on, tons of people took me for their little brother.) Neither of them went to the gym. They were just these genetically massive dudes. I came to discover that the Schroeders were the single craziest clan in skateboarding, by far. But I didn't know that at the time.

During his ride in the finals, Matthew fell off his board. This pissed him off immensely. Falling in the finals pretty much guaranteed you weren't going to come close to winning. So then, in a spontaneous fit of pure animal aggression, Matthew headed up the rail of one of the miniramps and continued his ride up off the miniramp course, onto a vert ramp that was right next to it. He then rode up to the rail of the vert ramp, and jumped off, back onto the miniramp. This was about a twenty-five-foot jump.

Let me pause for a second and remind you, this was the late '80s. This was not on ESPN. It wasn't about TV time and sponsors. This was just about the love for skateboarding, and being a lunatic, and pushing yourself as far as you could go. I was going insane. Everybody was. This was not a skater we were watching—this was a reincarnated barbarian warlord.

On his way flying back down, Matthew missed the transition and landed in the flat. (For the nonskateboarders out there, that's the flat bit of the ramp, in the middle. Hence the name.) With the force of this landing, I saw the bottom of the ramp break underneath Matthew's board a second before his body mercilessly slammed. He picked his board up and tried to skate it, but pretty much every part if it had been destroyed on impact.

As Matthew was wreaking havoc, I noticed that the fence I was standing behind had started moving. Swaying. Bending over, back and forth. I look over, and it's Ben Schroeder, watching his brother. What Matthew had just done provoked this one-man riot of happiness inside of Ben. We'd all been drinking a little bit, mind you, but now Ben was smashing the fence over, to storm onto the ramp and tackle his brother. He wasn't even consciously doing what he was doing—it was a physical reaction that came over him, to honor the warrior mind-set that Matthew had just channeled.

This was primal shit that was happening here. My mind was

blown. For the first time, I had witnessed what you might call the real men among skateboarders. It was very inspirational.

I slept under the ramp that night.

It was a two-day contest. My turn came up the next day. It was my first contest on a miniramp. I don't remember how I did, so it obviously wasn't too spectacular. No one had any idea who I was. I remember Dave Duncan, then and now the Voice of Skateboarding, announcing my name as Jason "Elise," like the girl's name.

That night, me and Gary had enough money to stay in a cheap motel—maybe like a forty-bucker. As we were walking there from the ramp, I remember seeing a donut store. To me, where I was coming from, this was amazing. Shocking Asia—a store that only sells *donuts*? You have got to be shitting me. And then Ben Schroeder—one of the He-Man twins—drove by in his white Bronco. Since Ben was driving a brand-new, glistening American car, that meant, in my mind, that he was obviously extremely rich.

He recognized us from the event and invited us to a party, where we all did some drinking. I think maybe Gary had met Ben the first time Gary came to America.

After that night, Ben's family took us in. Me and Gary were like a couple of hobbits living among giants. Just like Ben and his brother, everything about the Schroeder family was gigantic. Ben's parents had a massive house, maybe an hour inland from the ocean. A great big place loaded with massive people. Ben's parents had tons of their own kids, and there was a sister that had even more kids. Everyone there was bigger than me. The dad's a massive dude that worked for NASA. The mom's got a few inches on me, too. They had a massive fridge. A massive door with massive door handles. Massive stairs. I felt like a tiny little person. Like my two-year-old son, Tiger, trying to wrap my little person hands around their massive soda glasses. Ben's

dad took me to my first Costco, where he bought some massive groceries. That place blew my mind.

Straightaway, Gary started bumming Ben out. Gary had a very
strategic approach to skating, and to life. Looking back on it, he was
ahead of his time. Nowadays most skaters look at things the way Gary
did back then. Like a job. Like a business. But Ben was antiplanning.
Antistrategy. To him, if you went skating and you didn't have a hangover, that meant you were a pussy.

Guess which one of those guys I ended up going along with?
As me and Ben became close, my friendship with Gary pretty much
ended, and we went our separate ways for the rest of the trip. Although
Ben was a few years older than me, we got tighter and tighter, real
quick. His attitude toward life rubbed off on me fast, and not in a
good way. More than anything else, that's where this punk rock thing
of mine came from. Ben didn't mean to turn me into a monster. It
wasn't his fault. I was already naturally crazy. He didn't do that. I just
loved skateboarding, and I wanted to push myself. I didn't care what
happened to me. That ride his brother took at the Vans contest, that
was the kind of guy I now wanted to become. The daredevil. The guy
that everyone else on the ramp was afraid of.

Ben took me under his wing. I became a drinker. A rager.
I started trying to be a mini Ben Schroeder. Whereas before I had
been imitating Gregor and Lee, back in Australia, and their very disciplined lifestyle, now I was taking my cue from Ben. I was basically
living at his house, and trying to be him.

Ben was the first grown man to tell me that he loved me. We
were smoking weed out of a Budweiser can in his car, up on the top of
the mountains in Visalia, California, and he just said it, while exhal-
ing a hit. "I love you, man." I pretended I didn't hear him. I thought he
was gay or something. Later on, I realized that we did love each other,

and that didn't mean he wanted to try to bone me. When I put that together, I remember consciously planning to get drunk some other time and tell him I loved him, too. At that moment, though, I didn't say anything. I just powered through and stayed focused on the weed.

Along with Ben and a couple of the other Schroeders, we continued on to Mission Beach, down in San Diego. What's that summer party thing you guys do? Spring break? I didn't know anything about it. We don't have anything like that in Australia. I was looking around, thinking, *Wait, you guys don't have to go to school? Your parents flew you from fucking Texas or wherever to spend two weeks in your house on the beach? Who are all you spoiled motherfuckers?*

Those two weeks were the greatest time of my life to that point. Mission Beach was, to put it mildly, a massive whore fest. I had sex with a disgusting amount of girls. I was doing okay in Australia, but not like this. It was the accent. And I had my flowing blond locks. I don't think I've ever been more attractive in my entire life than when I got off the plane here. It's all been steadily downhill since. As I've lost my outback pizzazz, I have slowly become more and more hideous to American women.

My first threesome was in Mission Beach. With a couple of Italian girls that couldn't speak English. They had hairy armpits. I went back to their hotel room, and the way I explained that I wanted to bone them was by doing the old sticking-your-finger-in-the-hole bit. The universal language of jamming. I was like, "Me? You?" They were like, "Ohhhh," and then they giggled and nodded their heads. And that's how it went down. Just that easy.

Another time I was riding in the back of a Cadillac, laying sideways and boning a chick. She was straddling me. Ben was in the passenger seat. The girl's *mother* was driving, taking us from one random keg party to the next one, and we made no attempt to hide what was going on. At traffic lights and stop signs, onlookers were cheering me on. Midpump, I threw a thumbs-up out the window, to confirm that, yes, indeed, this chick is bouncing up and down on my penis. Thank you, America! Great to be here!

There were girls everywhere. I was blown away by all the blond-headed chicks. They called me F.F.—Fucking Foreigner. I was famous, for those two weeks at least. Walking on the beach, people would be yelling at me—"F.F.! F.F.!" All the time.

It was amazing how much mileage you could get out of the whole Australia thing. I discovered that my accent was incredibly entertaining to people. As soon as I opened my mouth, girls were really, really into it. Without even planning to, I made up a story, drunk, that soon became pretty legendary: "Drop Bears." Rabid koala bears that will drop from trees and attack you. I was always good at making up stories. It was hilarious.

I made up the story one time at a party, and then I would add more to it every time. People don't know—they think koalas are all cuddly and shit, but if a koala wanted to fuck you up, you could die. It's like trying to pick up a bobcat. It will slice you up. And they make this noise, a roar, like a monster. All of that is true.

What I added was that there were these koalas—drop bears— that hang out in the trees and then drop down and eat your face. "Drop bears," I would be telling some dumb hot chicks. "I've seen them a million times. You've gotta watch out." My friends would sit there trying not to laugh as another batch of strangers went for it. Several times after that, after some stranger figured out I was Australian, they asked *me* if *I* had ever been attacked by a drop bear. So many people had passed that dumb story on, it actually came around back to me.

The party never stopped during those two weeks of spring

break. We were at a house party one night, and there was this big rope attached to the roof and a pole sticking out the front of the house. Some guy was saying he was gonna swing off this rope, out on to the boardwalk. And people were yelling, "Do it! Do it!" But the guy just wouldn't commit. Most likely because he was a massive pussy. So I was standing there watching him, and I just grabbed the rope and swung off myself, past the boardwalk and all the way out onto the beach. Some girl came out when I was on the beach and stripped down to nothing and did a dance for me, while everybody was cheering. A pretty big crowd—maybe two hundred people. And then I boned her, as everyone kept on cheering.

It all seems a little impossible, thinking back, but I was there. This all happened. I have witnesses. This was a gross time, sure. But I didn't care. I was having a fucking ball. I was just skateboarding every day and partying every night. No job. No parents. No one to tell me to do anything. Drinking and taking experimental drugs. We raged everywhere we went, kicking things, and generally being disrespectful little assholes. People would yell at us, out their windows, "Hey, man, you can't break my house!" "Sorry, bro!" We'd laugh, and then move along, and rampage and destroy some more shit somewhere else.

I would say hello to some hot blond chick, have sex with her in some strange bed, and then move on to the next adventure. Over and over again. Boning people on the beach, then sleeping there, so drunk I'd be snoring with sand inside my mouth. The beach crew telling us we needed to get the fuck out of there in the morning. It was just like, what can't I do? How far can I take this? I would disappear—no money, no nothing—and then find Ben again, a day later, somewhere on the boardwalk. "Hey, Ben, I'm hungry," I'd say, and he would grab a burger out of somebody's hands and give it to me. Like I was a baby pigeon. Nobody fucked with Ben.

The first night I arrived in Mission Beach, at a surf shop on the boardwalk, I temporarily fell in love with this space-age superhot hippie chick called Sunny. We were like a serious boyfriend and girlfriend for about three days, and then: poof. Never saw her again. I ran back into the Schroeders at a party, after Sunny disappeared. I think Ben was impressed by how I had gone off with this chick, with no money to speak of—you know, my casual disregard for life and death—and now here I was, back at the next keg party, ready for the next round.

In the meantime, Sunny had given me mushrooms. I was watching a soccer game at her house, with all these weird other people there. She was being very comforting, patting me, like a den mother. One minute I was watching the game, and then I felt my head start to spontaneously pull off in a different direction, up and away. Just like that, I was gone, into the spirit world.

For a whole entire day, I didn't know who I was, or what I was doing, but I was not on this planet. The next thing I remember was waking up in a bed the next morning, staring at this crystal that was in my hand. At that moment, I probably believed that it gave me mystical powers. This Sunny chick did, for sure. When I went back to Lance Mountain's ramp, I skated with no T-shirt on. Just a leather necklace, with the crystal dangling off it.

Beyond the drugs and destruction and magical fairy fuck-buddies—and even if I was occasionally skating with a crystal dangling across my bare chest—I was still learning my three tricks a day, just like Lance Mountain had told me to. That was the thing I told myself I needed to accomplish, day in and day out, for the whole six months. Other skaters would say, "Hey, have you tried this?" And they'd show me something. And then I'd just do it, like that. That was the most ability I'd ever felt inside myself, for anything. At least until radio came along. Later on, the tricks get harder, and it gets harder to get them dialed. But when you don't know anything, it's easy to learn a lot in a hurry, and that gets addictive.

After our Mission Beach adventure, me and Ben headed up to the San Francisco Bay area. I lived in the San Jose Warehouse and learned billions of tricks. That's where I got my first American sponsor, Santa Cruz. (Even though that one ended as soon as I went back home.) That's also where I slept with my first African American woman. Over the years there have been tons of black chicks, but that opportunity had never presented itself back home. I think I've always been very color-blind when it comes to people. I don't ever remember any racism being around when I was growing up. If it was, it went right over my head.

Anyway, I was at this party up by San Francisco, and I snuck off into a closet with this nice African American lady. We were in there, and then Lance and all these other people were trying to open the door. You know, "What are you two doing in there?" Being jackasses. And I'm like, "Shut the door! Shut the door!" They were all laughing at me for having sex in a closet. I thought it was awesome.

There was another girl I met who lived in San Jose. She went out with more than one pro skater, both before and after I passed through town. She had a house. That was the first time I ever saw a lava lamp. She taught me how to lick her cookie. We spent hours in her room, having sex, and her teaching me stuff about oral sex.

She said I had a huge penis. I remember not believing her at all. I thought she was such a pro—telling me how big my dick was. *That's an angle,* I thought. *That's a move. I've seen my old man's dick, and if mine is big, then you should see* him. One day in a supermarket, she just opened her mouth and said, "Don't you think ugly people are annoying?" Actually, no, I didn't. And I was pretty sure that thinking that made her a cunt. Although I didn't say it at the time, that was the end of that relationship.

Not long before my visa was up, I was at a party in San Francisco with Ben Schroeder. I was at some house, putting metal things in the microwave. Flicking Ajax around the kitchen. Just generally being an asshole. A massive skinhead with a scar from one side of his neck to the other came in. "What the fuck are you guys doing?"

I didn't hesitate to answer: "Partying."

And just like that, there went my window to get out of that one. In about two seconds, my chance to apologize had passed. He punched me in the face. I went down. He started kicking me in the stomach. Really good ones, too. I was wasted, but these blows were definitely registering.

Luckily Ben was around. Ben was like six foot six, but the skinhead dude didn't blink. So then they went at it. Ben had him by the ankles, swinging him around the house, smashing the skinhead into stuff headfirst. And then Ben grabbed him by the neck and held him out over the balcony. They were eye to eye. Still, there was no quit in the skinhead. He said, "Do it, you pussy." Luckily some other guys grabbed the dude before Ben could drop him. They held him down while me and Ben left. On the way out, in the corridor, I started puking blood from all the kicks. I definitely deserved that.

Ben was in a crazy car crash, maybe four years after we met. He fell asleep in the back of a truck, on a highway. He should have died. He was in a coma, and he lost a piece of his nose and his sense of smell. That was kind of the end of his career. Later on, as I got more focused on becoming an accomplished pro skateboarder, and started making money, and wearing shiny shit, and hanging out with some of the characters I came to be associated with, to Ben, I think I became a sellout. To him, trying to make a career out of being a skateboarder was a pussy thing to do. We're still friends, but when I see him, I can tell I turned out to be a bit of a disappointment.

That first six-month visa, I went to America a pasty little shit with scraggly hair. But I had a big growing spurt when I was there. I came back six inches taller—taller than my father—with long golden locks.

When I went back home, all I was thinking was: I need to get back to America. Immediately.

6.

BUT THEN I HAD TO GO
BACK TO AUSTRALIA

When I went to America, I think everyone back home knew I had the potential to be the best skateboarder in Australia. Everyone except me, maybe. But I don't think anybody thought I was going to get as far as I did, as fast as I did. I came back, and forget Australia, I was better than half the people in America. I had learned my three tricks a day for six straight months. That was my thing. Grow. Get faster. Beat everyone. It was my obsession. If I'd learned two tricks in a day, I couldn't leave the ramp until I got the third one down.

I've never worked harder at anything in my life. My generation was all about pushing the game. Pushing each other. We wanted to show people that we could do way more with our skateboards than anyone could possibly imagine. The end result was the greatest leap forward that skateboarding had ever seen.

I would work on trying to make tricks for hours at a time. Same thing, over and over and over again. And I just refused to do pussy tricks. I only did big stuff. Bangers. So usually that meant if I had a new trick I wanted to make, and I fucked it up, I was gonna get hurt. And then that would make me scared. And then I would get angry for being scared. And then if I didn't make a trick, I would be so pissed off I'd throw a fit. It's a bad habit. But when you got to a certain level, it became the thing you did. A lot of us.

At times, I would try the same shit, over and over, for maybe three straight days at a time. You know how frustrating it is to do that and still not be able to land the trick? I would get so pissed I would break anything I could get my hands on. Snap my board. Snap my helmet. Punch walls. Kick my shoes off into the bushes, and then just walk off in socks, shorts, and a shirt, and sit in the bushes for an hour and cry. Not talk to anyone for days at a time.

I wanted to be good so badly. There was no tomorrow. The only thing was making that trick. For years and years, that was my daily existence. Pushing myself meant I had to bounce back from horrific injuries. Every pro skateboarder does. Pain is part of the bargain. You break something, and then you heal, and then you slam on it and you break it all over again. You need to tell your brain to tell your body to just deal with it. I have a pretty high threshold for pain. I can take a hit. I learned that early.

I believe it's possible that I am part Fijian. Although she never knew it growing up, my mother was adopted by her real mother's sister. Many, many years later, probably when I was in my twenties, the woman that raised my mother revealed the secret before she died. When my mum found out the truth, her real mother didn't even want to meet her. That fucked with my mum a little bit, for sure.

Grandma was an alcoholic, we're told. Grandma was also a bit of a whore, apparently. Because it turns out my mother has approximately twenty-seven brothers and sisters. Some of them look like regular Australians. But some of them are massive Samoans. I saw a birth certificate. It said my grandfather is from Fiji. The only thing that makes me believe it might be possible is that I do have a thick head. I have thick bones. It is hard to knock me out.

Doctors have told me to stop skateboarding a million times. For example, after skating for a few years, my shoulder kept coming out of the socket. It was no big deal—I used to pull it out at parties, for fun. But then one day, after my first trip to America, I landed on it while I was skating and pulled it out even more. I remember walking to the hospital holding my arms over my head, crying. The doctor told me I would never skate again. This is before anybody would have surgeries to keep skating, and all that. I remember thinking, *It's over. I'm never gonna skate again. I can't go to the States, ever again.*

The next day at work, at Ellistronics, I cried. Someone was consoling me. "At least you still have a job." Of course I knew he was trying to help. But I felt immediate hatred for this person. His name was Tom. He was a fucking prick. He was working there illegally, and he used to sell Rolexes on the side. I remember thinking, *Fuck that. I'm lifting weights until my shoulder stays in there. Because I am not working with you for the rest of my life, you bastard.*

One time I shattered my wrist so bad, my hand got stuck all the way back against my arm. Pointing in the exact *wrong* direction. My knuckle was literally touching the top of my forearm. I quickly grabbed it and pulled it back more or less into place, but it was really wobbly. The pain was so bad I could barely get off the ramp. Then I walked to the hospital. And when I got there, another doctor informed me my skateboarding career was over. After a while, you just learned to ignore them.

I ended up bonding with my brothers, Stevie and Lee, over injuries. As they grew up a bit, and got into their own moronic and dangerous activities, we started keeping score. Who had the most stitches. Who had the most broken bones. Stuff like that. I probably started it. Lee was always headbutting stuff with that massive dome of his, so he always had stitches on his head. But Stevie won. He slid off the roof of a tin fence and cut his ass all the way up and down. There was no catching up with him after that.

For a couple of years, after my first tourist visa in the United States ran out, my life was six months in America, and then six months home, scraping together the money for a ticket to get my ass back to the States. It was just about getting the ticket. I never came with any cash. The second trip, my dad gave me a credit card, to prove to Customs I had money, but only because I promised him I would cut the card up and throw it in the trash as soon as I left the airport.

When I was back in Australia during those years, life was just skating with that Gregor and Lee group. They pretty much *were* skateboarding in Australia. It's fair to say they felt they had created a monster. I was out from under their wing. While I was gone, I had become the thing they hated and feared most. Their thing was to be hard-core. Don't be some glam pussy. At first, I had prided myself on being as hard-core as them. I didn't smoke. I didn't drink. I slept under the ramp. I slept in the hallway at their apartment. They didn't even have mattresses—that's how ghetto they were. But then all of a sudden I had long hair, and I'd been to America, and I was drinking, and getting laid, and outskating everyone. So I see their point. I was annoying. I came back cocky as a motherfucker.

That's where my whole "I'm awesome" thing came from. No one else in my family was like that. I never heard my dad talk that way. You wouldn't say my family is shy, but they didn't do any boasting. That's the way most Australians are. My brother, Lee, got into motocross later on, and I think he became good at it because of me. I'd only see him a couple times a year, but in the little bit that we would talk, my message to him was: The Ellis family can do anything. We are the best at everything. If you want to rule at moto, simply go out every day, and you will be the best at it. Look at me—I'm the best. Dad is, too. I guess skateboarding opened me up. With ability came confidence. In everything.

I was the best skateboarder in Australia. By far. It wasn't even an argument anymore. In skateboarding, the first thing you shoot for is getting sponsored, which I accomplished by the time I was sixteen. (Hardcore paid me $166 every three months. I'd love to know how they worked out that exact figure.) But you aren't really a pro skater until you enter a pro contest. I had made up my mind I wasn't gonna do that until I won an amateur contest in America. I was good enough to be pro way before I knew it. I knew I was gonna be pro someday—I loved it so much—but I think I had a low self-opinion. I just looked at the other pros as sort of untouchable. Lance Mountain. Chris Miller. Tony Hawk. It was hard for me to face the fact that I could actually be a part of that. That's me, in a nutshell: I think I'm awesome, but I also think I'm a piece of shit. Back and forth, all day long.

The big annual contest, the Ramp Riot, was getting to be a real thing. All the American pros came over to it. It was at my home ramp, Prahran. A forty-foot-wide ramp, which was a massive deal. For some reason, they made Australians and New Zealanders practice in the same heat at this contest. And for some reason, that day, Gregor and Lee just snapped. They wanted to fight me. Lee was way bigger than me, and he said, "Just so you know, Goober, if you roll in, I'm gonna smash your fucking face in." I wasn't sure I heard him right. So he repeated himself. "You touch this fucking ramp, I'll fucking kill ya."

He said the same thing to two other guys. Both of them got off the ramp and didn't skate. Who knows what they did to piss him off that bad. Who knows what *I* did, really.

I dropped in. As soon as I did, Gregor dropped in, too. Coming after me.

This was a long ramp, remember. I did a Frontside Grind, going across the whole ramp. Gregor did a 50-50—*at* me—straightaway, from the other side, because he saw I wasn't gonna leave.

This was the practice session for the biggest contest I'd ever been in. The winner is the Australasian champion (which basically just means Australia and New Zealand). So I don't give a fuck. I'm not going anywhere. Beat me up, cocksucker. I'm mid-Frontside, and he's in the middle of a 50-50, and as we pass, he tries to punch me! As I see him coming, I lean back and feel his hand whizzing past my face.

And then I went up the other side, and did a 50-50, and, as I did that, Lee kicked underneath my board, but somehow I stayed on my feet and made it, and then came in and did another 50-50. Meanwhile, Gregor did a Frontside Grind toward me. He was a little bit ahead of me. He shot off, and I shot off behind him. And while both of us are in the air, Gregor turned around, with his board in his hand, and threw the board at my face. I had my hand up, and it bounced off me, and then I did a couple more tricks. Which was a humongous Fuck You to them. Both of them were full-grown men. Ten years older than me. And now they have just tried to beat me up, on the ramp, during a practice session, in front of all the pros. Naturally, everyone was like, "What the fuck are these two dudes doing?"

I wish I could say I shoved that in their faces at the contest. I was better than their best guy, Gary . . . but not that time. It was Gary's night. He beat me fair and square. It was the last time I lost the Ramp Riot.

But Gary winning wasn't the end of it. Around this time, Lee had just started drinking. That night, Lee also took acid, and Gregor told him to come to my hotel room and beat the shit out of me. Luckily, that plan did not succeed, mainly because Ben Schroeder is massive, and he kept Lee from even getting inside my room.

The first time I won the Ramp Riot.
I became the Australasian champion, won four grand,
and blew all of the money as quickly and as stupidly as possible.

Lee left, thank God, but all night long, I had to watch where I was going. We were never really cool after that, until years later, when I was a legitimate pro, and had been for a long time. Even then, he never really explained why him and Gregor had both wanted to beat me down. He was just like, "Ah fuck, Goob. You know how it is."

I was eighteen when all this happened. This was two or three years after I met them. I hated them, and they hated me. I hated Hardcore, the company they worked for, and Hardcore hated me. But Hardcore ran skateboarding in Australia, and I was the best guy, so unfortunately I was still affiliated with them for years to come. But in my mind, other than a couple of friends, I was just solo.

I won the Ramp Riot the next year. I won four thousand dollars. I went to the guitar store and bought a twelve-string guitar for like eight hundred bucks, and I had no idea that you had to tune it. So once it went out of tune, I stopped playing it. I went to a restaurant with my friends, and we had bottles of red wine, and we ate dinner, and I remember the bill was a hundred dollars. And I paid for it. Everyone was like, "You are blazing, dude!" I spent the whole four grand in a couple months. Stickers and Metallica patches and shit. Fuck, I don't even know what else.

My old man never said anything about the money. Ever. I had four thousand dollars cash, and then it was gone, and then it was time to go get another job. My brother Lee saves money. Always has. I never did. No one ever told me to. No one asked me for anything. I always lived my own life. My stepmum wasn't even part of my life. She still just wanted me to get the fuck out of there. That was the feeling I got.

The Marilyn Monroe lookalike from the Snake Pit gave me the trophy when I won the Ramp Riot. When I came back to Australia, she had come over my parents' house and cooked me a roast. And then I licked her cookie on the couch, using all the skills I'd picked up from the chick with the lava lamp in San Jose. That was the day the Marilyn chick fell in love with me. For years and years she would cry over me. Ten years older than me, and she was harassing me. She wanted to marry me and stuff.

She was the first person who cried when I had sex with her. It was terrifying. The only time I had seen a full-grown woman cry was maybe if someone had died or something. I was totally not ready for that level of emotion in a sexual relationship. I was just having fun. One time, during sex, I howled in Marilyn's ass, on a rooftop. Like a wolf. I'm not sure what inspired me to do that. I think maybe it was mushrooms.

Things also picked up where they left off with Misty, my dad's friend's wife. Those couple of encounters from before I left began an affair that went on for years. I would go out, and if I couldn't get laid, I would call her and go over to her house. Me and Misty went on forever. Her and her husband, Roger, got a divorce. I ended up being friends with her kids. I taught her son to play the guitar. I was a little bit of a boyfriend, I guess.

It was awesome, but also a little creepy. I mean, she had changed my diapers when I was a baby. She was like a member of the family. One time, she picked me up at a train station, blew me in the car, and then we walked in my parents' house together. While I went to my room, she poured a glass of chardonnay and started chatting with Marn like nothing had happened. It was weird. I found out way too much about the family, because Misty would tell me. What Marn used to do. What Dad *was* doing.

There were all kinds of insane angles to the situation. One night I was at a club, and there was this announcement. "Jason Ellis, emergency phone call." I assumed it was something serious. I go to the phone, panicked. "Hello?" It was Misty's youngest sister. "It's Tracie.

I'm at Misty's house. You should come over." "Okay," I said. "That sounds kind of cool. But I'm still out."

"I'll come and get you."

And so Tracie comes to this club. Chasers, it was called. And she takes me in a taxi, headed back to Misty's. And then she says we should pull off on the beach. She was married to Alan, the dude that I built my family's vacation home with, in a place called Tanjil Bren. One of my dad's closest friends. I loved him.

And I fucked his wife.

And then I went back to Misty's, and I fucked Misty, and Misty had no idea that me and her sister had stopped off on the way there.

Misty was in love with me. And I wasn't in love with anybody. I was a teenage dude. I loved skateboarding. And maybe Metallica. That was pretty much the list. Me and Misty went on until eventually my stepmum got wind of everything and confronted me. "Do you love her?" she asked. Wow. She wasn't getting this at all. She had no idea. This was ludicrous. "Come on, Jason. You can admit it if you're in love with her. It's okay."

"Marn, I'm just fucking her."

I mean, I wasn't going to get into details during this particular conversation. But this chick was doing things sexually that I'd never seen before. This is a grown-ass woman. She was hot. She had fake tits and plastic surgery. She was an aerobics instructor.

So then, before I know it, Marn's calling her. I'm on the phone with Misty, and then I had to give the phone to my stepmother. Marn is telling Misty she's disgusted. Misty is telling Marn that she's in love, and *you don't understand,* and all that. And I'm standing by the phone, thinking *Why am I involved with this? Please. I didn't mean to do any of it.*

I remember I was scared of Roger, Misty's husband. I thought he hated me. I thought he wanted to fight me. I was so bummed out. I thought I was responsible for breaking them up. Misty would always tell me that wasn't the case. Marn still isn't friends with Misty, to this day, because of all this. They had been best friends. At the time, I remember thinking it was a stupid thing to fight over. That they should just get over it. But I guess that wasn't the way they saw it.

I believe, at the time, all this stuff made me think a little less of women. At least, it made me think that they were all just like men—driven to have sex constantly, and not necessarily to be in faithful relationships.

That for sure affected the way things went with Rachel, a girl I met right around then. Rachel and I met at a skate ramp. I thought she was hot, so I skated over to say hello. Cruising over to look like a champ. And then of course I hit a stone and ate shit in front of her. She would always bring that up, for years to come. What I didn't know was that at home, in her room, she had a whole wall of pictures of me. Tony Hawk had a wall. I had a wall. I think maybe Chris Miller had one, too. She was such a skateboard rat. She actually really appreciated the sport. I'll say that for her.

Once we started seeing each other, Rachel stayed in my life for almost a decade. People thought we were exactly the same. We could go bong rip for bong rip, beer for beer. She eventually became a centerfold model in Australia. She looked like Cindy Crawford, only with massive real boobs. She was really hot, and I was a really good skateboarder. What more do you need in a relationship, right?

From the time I got back from the United States that first time, partying became more and more a part of my existence. From time to time, I would decide to get really sober and really focused. I would commit to some crazy regimen, like eating only fish and rice for three straight months, or something like that, because I maybe heard that was good for you. But for the most part, I was on the Ben Schroeder program of drinking a ton and going for it on the ramp. Rachel was fully on board with that game plan.

I also hung out a lot in those days with my friend John Finlay. Fin and I used to get drunk and fight each other. Not, like, punch each other in the face. Not for real. Fin would never really fight a guy. And neither would I. But we would get so drunk that we would smash each other's heads on the ground and stuff like that. I remember one time we were fighting each other. He was holding my hair, and I was holding his hair, and we were trying to smash each other's head on the wall. We both had our other hand on the wall, trying to not have our head caved in. Finally I moved his hand, and smashed his head on the wall, and cracked it open. He had kind of short hair, and I remember blood coming out. Down his ear. Down his face. I was like, "Dude, you are bleeding. Profusely."

We were a couple of drunk tough guys, so we didn't care that he was gushing blood. We were planning on a night out, though, and I was like, "Dude, you're not gonna get in a club with blood leaking out of your skull." Thinking quick, he grabbed a baseball cap and put it on. There you go. Problem solved.

And we left and went to the club, and some huge security guard dude wouldn't let us in because Fin had blood coming down his head. We made some sarcastic joke, and the bouncer slapped Fin right in the face. Hard. Fin went down. We just giggled and left. Returning violence didn't even cross our mind. If anything went down, it was people beating *us* up, because we were so drunk and obnoxious. Fin and I traded a lot of physical abuse back and forth. Because, if he got hurt, it didn't really *hurt* him. Just like me.

One time, me and Rachel were drinking and partying with Fin. I was skating on the Big Day Out tour, this huge traveling music festival they do every year in Australia. By then I had also discovered the wonders of ecstasy. It isn't too hard to figure out where all the drinking and drugs were coming from. When I was young, I did think that I needed to be wasted to be fun and outgoing. But probably even then, I could have told you I was also self-medicating. On this occasion, I was hanging out in a pool, and I was so blasted on ecstasy, I started talking to myself. I have no recollection of this fateful moment at all, but when I came out of my haze, Rachel was freaking the fuck out.

She told me I'd been talking to an imaginary friend. Mind you, I never had an imaginary friend when I was a kid, or anything like that. Apparently, me and this friend of mine had been talking about how I was molested. When I was little. Like five years old. Until that point, that wasn't something I consciously remembered. Fuck—I can even remember seeing abused people on *Oprah* and feeling bad for the poor bastards. It was buried down inside my mind. I guess the ecstasy somehow managed to dig it out.

I don't know what's the good way to take that information, but Rachel utterly lost her shit. She immediately called my mother. My mum knew what she was talking about. She told Rachel it had been a babysitter. A guy. An adult. Rachel decided on the spot that since I had been molested by a man, that made me gay. She kind of held on to that theory for years to come, actually.

I'm not really sure what else she told my mum. I'm not really sure what else my mum told her, either. At the time, it wasn't a subject that any of us were anxious to discuss any further. It kind of got swept under the rug.

To this day, I'm still trying to get straight answers about exactly what happened when I was a kid.

7.

MY THREE-YEAR
ENDLESS SUMMER

Starting when I was seventeen, I was constantly going back and forth between Australia and America. Six months here, and six months there. For three straight years, between America and Australia, I had an endless summer. But between the two places, I was living almost two different lives.

In Australia, after falling out with Gregor and Lee, I just had my little clique of people. There wasn't much of a vert scene, or a contest scene. It was mainly just street skaters. In America, there was still a vert scene, and that meant I had all these buddies to skate with all the time.

With Ben Schroeder, in America, we would drink a lot, and drink fast. But there were no drugs for me there, at least in the beginning. Meanwhile, we were pushing the limits in Australia way more when it came to partying. Ecstasy, speed, acid, mushrooms, shit like that. Every time it came down to the day before I was going back to America, it would be a vulgar display. I wouldn't even see my family. I would say good-bye the day before. Then me and my friends would rage all night, up until they took me to the airport. "Later, Ellis! Kick ass, you cunt!" When I was gone, maybe I would call home one time over the whole six months. "Hey, I'm alive." That was it.

Skateboarding in America was big enough to be its own little universe. We did not appreciate people who didn't skate. We looked at the whole non-pro-skater world approximately the same way a sixteen-year-old girl looks at her parents. Everyone who wasn't one of us was on the outside looking in. And once you were legit, it was like you got adopted into the family.

One time, pretty early on, I got driven up to Christian Hosoi's place in the Hollywood Hills. As great as Tony Hawk was (and is), Hosoi was the ultimate rock star of skateboarding. The whole time I was on his property, skating his personal ramp, Christian was inside the house. I'm not going to speculate on what he was doing in there, but by now his drug use around that time is pretty well known. Me and a bunch of other guys had been skating outside his mansion for a few hours when all of the sudden the door opens, and Hosoi comes flying out. No warm-up, cutoff shirt, bandannas hanging off him, and he just took one ride from hell. He did Frontside Ollie after Frontside Ollie, just to get more speed, which is nuts. (Sorry—more skate talk. But believe me, that *is* nuts.) He unleashed a couple of unbelievable tricks, then promptly flew off the side of the ramp and landed on his ass. When he tried to get up, he slipped and fell into his pool. Then he went back inside. Never said a word.

I really arrived in skateboarding in 1991. I was twenty. I had always said I needed to win an amateur contest before I entered any pro events. I finally won Linda Vista Am, down by San Diego. So then I went on a pro skate tour of Europe. I just barely scraped that trip together. I slept on hotel room floors, along with a bunch of other skaters.

I went to Munster, Germany, to the first pro event I entered. The Munster Cup, at the time, was the world title. Not one single person knew who I was. I've never been so nervous in my life. Danny Way had emerged as obviously the best skateboarder of the new breed. I was still nobody, down in Australia. A German dude named Titus was the biggest skateboarding distributor on the planet. He had a Lamborghini, and he would give the famous guys a ride in it. He held the contest. He would have every pro in the world there. Hundreds of people competed, and it went on for three days. It was a ginormous thing.

At that point, I could do Backside 540s and Tail Grab 540s. To put that in perspective, the only other person that could do a Tail Grab 540, as far as I knew, was Tony Hawk. That was the only documented Tail Grab 540 ever done. I had that, and I was waiting to show everybody in this contest. Turns out there was another guy there that had long blond hair. Very similar vibe entirely. Same age. And he could do Backside 540s and Tail Grab 540s. He was from Canada. His name is Rob "Sluggo" Boyce, the original Red Dragon. We both did Backside 540s and Tail Grab 540s in our ride. I think we both probably made two apiece, ever, and we both did them in that contest, along with every other trick we were doing. There's no way I could beat twenty-year-old me nowadays.

That's the day me and Sluggo met. (More on him and the Red

Dragons later.) I think he got sixth, and I got fifth. Tony Hawk won, Chris Miller got second, Steve Caballero got third, and Buck Smith got fourth. The only people that beat me were icons. I beat everybody else. I beat Danny Way.

I showed up as a nobody, and by the end of the three days, thousands of Germans recognized me. And so did everybody in skateboarding, from that point on.

It was truly awesome.

I don't remember how much money I got for fifth place. Probably nothing. But that allowed me to join the Planet Earth team. Chris Miller was one of the guys that started Planet Earth, and in my eyes Chris Miller was the man, so I took the deal. A deal that worked out to free skateboards. There was no paycheck. It was starting to become a pretty bleak time for vert skating. I, of course, was completely oblivious to that fact.

That night, to celebrate after the contest, I went to a bar. Jeff Kendall and all these legends were there. I grabbed a beer mug and smashed it over my head.

And then no one said anything.

Jeff broke the silence. He said, "Fuck yeah!" and then held a beer mug in front of me, and *BOOM!* I punched it. It shattered everywhere. Understandably, many of the people there did not know what to make of this display. "Yeah!" I yelled. And then I noticed my finger. To this day, I have the scar. Like sixteen stitches, through my hand. You could see the bone, and blood was shooting out in little spurts, over and over. The taxi wouldn't let me in. I had to put my hand in a plastic bag. And then Randy Janson, my team manager, took me to the hospital.

I was cursing everybody out. Just a drunk motherfucker. And then the doctor, who didn't speak English, came in. He stuck some needles in my finger, and I sobered up immediately. When he put the needle in, I remember thinking it was the most pain I'd ever been in. Which was saying something.

I probably got hurt more than anybody in skateboarding, for the kind of career I've had. I was never that great at skating, naturally. I just tried hard. I think I'm like twenty-five broken bones deep. I've been knocked out eight or nine times. Maybe ten. I don't know. A lot. I've had knee surgeries. Ankle surgeries. Snapped my tailbone off. Compound fractures. Broken toes. Separated shoulders. Internal bleeding. Swollen intestines. You name it. The works. For a while there, I was just permanently in a cast. I've broken my right wrist like eight times.

Despite what you might think, I don't really believe I have an amazingly high pain threshold. And I'm definitely not here to tell you that the painful experiences of my life have somehow made my body tougher. That's bullshit. Being a stocky guy in skateboarding meant I slammed harder than everyone else. The bigger the dude, the harder you fall. Simple as that. You *can* practice getting hit. Maybe some of the nerves do go dead a little. And who knows—maybe I really do have some thick Fijian bones in me. But mainly, if you want to make a trick bad enough, you'd be surprised what you'd be able to power through.

Following the Munster Cup—and my celebration at the bar afterward—I was in a sling. I had also popped the cartilage out of my knee, too, so I was limping, with the sling on. But I was still skating when we got to the next stop, Le Grand Bornand, some contest in France. I skated there on one arm and one leg.

That was the first time Tony Hawk ever talked to me, at Le Grand Bornand. Because I got fifth at the Munster Cup. I had a spark in my eye, you might say. I'm the fifth-best dude in the world. (That wasn't actually the case, mind you, but that's what I'm telling myself.) So now I'm thinking, *If I can get fifth . . . could I win? Could I beat this man? The god that is standing on the other side of the deck?* I dropped in at practice. I remember doing a Backside air, and I hear Tony's voice.

"Jason Ellis is gonna win the contest."

Tony Hawk was one of these people that didn't talk. It was like a Michael Jordan thing. At one point, he was so good, it might have been a little bit lonely for him. In those early days, if I was on the deck with him, and he said something to somebody—anybody—I was eavesdropping like crazy. Obviously pretending I'm not paying attention. But secretly obsessed. What does this man have to say?

Jason Ellis is gonna win the contest? What does he mean? Is he fucking with me? Does he actually, really think that? Could it be true?

Well . . . I only had one working arm at the time, and my knee was fucked. I didn't even qualify.

Knowing Tony now, he was just happy for me, that I'd done well. He was trying to give me a pat on the back, I think. There was no need for him to be intimidated by me. There was no way I was coming to get him. Ever.

There was a riot in the street after that contest. We were all out at some bars drinking heavily, and meanwhile Sluggo was breakdancing with these French people. He's good at it. He was the Canadian break-dance champion. I think he was some kind of Canadian gymnastic champion, too. He's also a professional snowboarder and a stuntman. We've had a lifelong competition with each other. I think I've officially won now, with the success of my radio show. He's into MMA now, too, but if we fought, I would kill him. Also, I've got more followers on Twitter. So, boom. Game over. Take that, Sluggo.

Anyway, Sluggo's break-dancing in France, and he did a helicopter, and some French dude kicked him. And then everybody went to beat him up, and there was this huge riot between the locals and the Americans. The mayor came out and told us, "If you guys don't go to your hotel rooms immediately, you will be arrested, and you will be put in jail for three days, minimum." We were all leaving the next day and heading to the Netherlands so that would have been bad for us.

Meanwhile, Craig Johnson, a pro skater, was in a bar. He had these dreadlocks, and they were tied up on the back of his head. He was playing pool, and the lights on the wall set fire to his dreads, more than once. Maybe the third time it happened, after he once again finished extinguishing his hair, he turned around and pulled the light out of the wall. The cord underneath came out of the plaster. And so he continued pulling it out, all the way around the wall. Fucked the place up pretty good. And then he ran out of there.

I was drunk out of my mind. People were stealing drinks, and then the riot police came. And they had the blockades, and the big plastic shields. I was in front of everybody else. I took my dick out and showed the police, and the crowd cheered at me, for sticking it to the man by putting my penis on display.

And then the tear gas bombs came, and everybody ran for their lives. I saw someone running with his T-shirt over his face, so I tied my shirt over my face. I could barely walk, with my knee, and the sling. A car came by. I couldn't run, so I grabbed on to the back of the car, and was just skidding away like that, holding on to the bumper.

Mark Gonzales, a pro skater, was standing on the back of the car. There was a photo—I think in *Thrasher* magazine—of this actual event. I'm in a blue flannel, hanging on to the back. And then Lee Ralph appears. Though he had been trying to kill me not that long ago, he was now my friend, and out of Australia and away from Gregor. Now Lee was in the party scene of skateboarding. Lee was yelling, "Fuck yeah, Ellis!" I reached out to shake hands with him, with the good hand, and as soon as I took that hand off the car, the bad hand let me down. I came right off and skidded, in like a scorpion pose, legs in the air, right on my face. And then I got up and ran off into the night.

From there the tour continued to Amsterdam, which quickly became one of my favorite places on earth. It's hard for anything to match Amsterdam. The first time I went there, as soon as I got off the train, I literally ran to the smoke shop. I told my team manager, "You check me in—I'll see you later."

I liked to smoke weed with tobacco. I went to the shop and said, "What's the strongest weed you've got?" The guy there pointed to the one he presumably referred all tourist idiots like myself to. "I'll have a gram of that!" I said. So I chopped the whole gram up, with tobacco, desperately, in a rush. I'm not even sitting down yet. I'm standing by the table, yelling orders at everyone. "Who's got papers? Who's got a bong? What are we doing here? You—light this joint up. You—load the bong while we smoke this joint." No one wanted any part of my tobacco/weed mix, which suited me just fine. I dumped all of it into a hookah, and I'm smoking it, thinking, *Man, this is the greatest country on the planet,* and then someone's like, "Hey, Ellis, have a space cake." And I'm like, "Space cake, what's that? Gimme that!" And I'm eating and smoking and I'm hungry as a mother-fucker, and then somebody tells me they have hash milk shakes. Hash milk shake? That's impossible! I was sure it would taste like shit, but actually, it was delicious, so down it goes! All right, now we're in business, let's go get some hookers!

But first, I wanted to roll a joint, because I'd never walked down the street in public, smoking weed. And I'm walking around, pur-posely hitting the joint when strangers are near me. "Hi there! Nice to see you. Just got here from Australia. Would you believe there is *mari-*

juana in this cigarette?" Like some kind of fucked-up Mick Dundee, unleashed in Amsterdam.

I'm on my way to the red light district when suddenly I start to second-guess myself. Wait—am I sure weed is really legal here? I start to believe that I've gotten that bit wrong, and that any second now, the authorities will be taking me away to rot in some filthy Dutch jail.

I decide I do not want the joint, so I get rid of it. Then I start getting suspicious about my shorts. I can feel a breeze on my knees, which makes me think they are unstylishly short. I catch my shirt in a reflection and realize I have become very fat. How have I not noticed that until *this very moment*? I'm getting very confused. I forget we're heading to the red light district, and all of a sudden I hear the sound of something tapping on glass. I turn around and am face-to-face with a withered old she-beast of a prostitute. She wanted a piece of me. I wanted out.

I bolted.

I was lost on the streets of Amsterdam. Alone. I couldn't find my hotel. I was sweating. I was scared. When I finally did find the hotel after an hour of wandering around, I got my team manager to let me in my room, where I promptly threw up. It wasn't even dark out yet, but I went fetal in the bed, passed out, and slept through to the next morning.

I got my Metallica tattoo on that first Amsterdam trip from Hanky Panky, a famous artist. Hanky Panky rolled up a magazine and said, "If you move, I'll crack you in the head with this." I was afraid to flinch when he put the gun on my skin, on my upper right leg. I already had a bunch of animal tattoos at that point. I got all those for motivation. Fly like an eagle. The reflexes of a snake. The agility of a cat. Very cheesy shit, but whatever. I've always loved animals, because of my mum. My mum is one of those crazy animal people. She owns a pet-minding service, still. People always used to put puppies out the front of the house, because they knew she'd take care of them. She was famous for that. She always had tons of dogs and cats. I always slept with like eight dogs and sixteen cats all around me. Fur everywhere.

Right after I got the tattoo, I got pushed into a room with a hooker by Randy Janson, my team manager. He paid for it. I had his money in my hand, and she took it. I may have been itching to meet some hookers when I was at the hash bar, but by the time it actually happened I was really nervous. Scared. I didn't want to do it, and I was just happy when it was over. Everybody cheered when I came out. Now I was a man, apparently. Metallica tattoo, and my first prostitute. Big day. I called my dad to tell him.

That was the first Amsterdam trip. That was before that place made me evolve into a creepy monster on sight.

BEING ON PLANET EARTH, WHEN we got back to America, I stayed at Chris Miller's house for a while. It's funny—to him, I was this mild-mannered guy. I was straight edge the whole time I was there, which was only for a month or two. I was always trying to quit drinking. I would go through my phases of being really healthy. The partying tended to come in spurts, too.

In Sacramento, I was getting ready for a contest and still aiming to take my place among the greats of skateboarding. I had a really good session the day before. But somewhere in there I tore my ACL. I had no idea what an ACL was—it's a ligament in your knee, by the way—so I iced it a bunch and then tried to skate, but I could barely stand. I was so bummed out. I was shattered. No contest for me.

And then, in the hotel room the next day, we had a big party. Sergie Ventura had showed up in a convertible Mustang, with Christian Hosoi and this really hot blond chick. And now, in his hand, he had a sheet of acid which was about the size of a piece of computer paper. We had no idea where it came from. Clearly, there was enough for everyone, but I wasn't skating anymore that weekend, so I grabbed it out of his hand and took a huge bite out of it. Everyone could have gotten mad at me for taking all the drugs, but I think they were more taken aback at what an outrageously stupid thing it was to do. I brushed them off. "Ah, mate, we do that all the time in Australia." Which was utterly not true. I'd done acid, but not in anything like this sort of volume. I'd never even *seen* a sheet of acid before.

This skater named Remy Stratton tried to walk with my crutches, and he broke them both in half. So I was drunk, and I was on acid, and I was dragging this dead leg around, trying to keep up with everybody.

I ended up sitting in a car with a skater named Sean Miller, a great guy who's since passed away, unfortunately. He was also on acid. We were both holding some crystals we had found—the sorts of things that always seem to magically turn up when you're on heavy-duty psychedelic drugs. We tapped them together, and at the exact same moment some sprinklers outside the car came on, which was pretty trippy. We were talking for a while, and then we tapped the crystals again and the sprinklers turned off. This convinced us we possessed magical powers, which freaked us both out, so we decided to get the fuck out of there.

Somewhere along the way, I met up with the chick that had come with Sergie, and I got her into the room I was sharing with Alphonzo Rawls. Poor Alph—he was kind of a nerdy guy who was actually more focused on his skateboarding than partying. What a loser. My stamina was pretty impressive on that acid. I came out of there very sweaty and ran right into Sergie. He is the sweetest dude ever. I've never seen him angry in my whole life. He couldn't care less that I stole all the acid *and* his woman. He was like, "Yeah, Ellis, you got that chick?!"

Later that night, everyone had gone to sleep, and me and Sean are out in the corridors, smashing shit. The guy who owned the parent company for Planet Earth, my sponsor, finally came out. "Who the fuck is out here?" Me and Sean pinned ourselves up against the wall. I was shaking. Almost crying. "What the fuck are you guys doing!?" he said. He slammed the door to his hotel room and I remember thinking, *Well, I'm not on Planet Earth anymore.* I figured that meant I had nothing to lose, so we decided to trash the place even more.

I punched a fire alarm. Everyone had to come out of their rooms. Sean told me to shut the fuck up about everything so that's what I did.

They never figured out it was me. Somehow, at the end of that, I was still sponsored by Planet Earth.

8.

FUCK YOU

ROLLERBLADERS

Timing is everything. No matter how many times I went to America, I always believed that the next trip would be the one that would establish me as a pro skater for good. I believed it the first time. And then again the second time. But I still didn't become a huge star. I didn't have a paycheck.

Third time's a charm, I told myself.

Nope.

I thought the skateboarding industry was just going to get better and better. I had no idea that vert skating was dying. Not just for me.

For everyone. In the early to mid '90s, by the time I was in my early twenties, Tony Hawk was barely making any money. Street skating was taking over. In skate videos, vert parts had come to be known as the "fast-forward parts." They wouldn't even put us in a fucking magazine. Vert skating and street skating are two completely different beasts. That's probably hard to understand if you're not in skateboarding, but I have more in common with motocross dudes than I do with street skaters. Moto dudes go fast. They go big. They jump shit. Street skating has none of that. No disrespect, but what street skating offers is not what attracted me to the sport in the first place.

There was no money in vert skating. Even to me it was obvious that going back to America a fourth time was pointless.

In the end, when I was cool—when I was absolutely as good as I was going to get—vert skateboarding wasn't. And when it got cool again, a few years later, I was still around, but I was too wasted, and my heyday was over.

After I had gotten fifth at the World Cup in Germany, and I got sponsored by Planet Earth, I was like, "Do I get a pro model skateboard now?" And Chris Miller told me no, because I was a vert skater, and that meant it wouldn't sell. So now I was back in Australia, getting free boards instead of a paycheck. I think I got four boards a month—not even enough so I could sell a few to make some spending money.

These were dark days. I won a contest called the Australasian High Air Masters. I think the winner was supposed to get six grand, and a trip to the Brazilian X Games. I could give a fuck about the Brazilian X Games, but the money and a trip sounded nice. We were all going after it hard. Instead they gave me a trophy. I got the organizer's number and called him. He didn't see what the big deal was. "Aw, there was never any money in it," he said. I was like, "You announced to the crowd that I had won all this money, and now you are telling me there's no money?" And he informed me that, yes, indeed, that was the deal. I was going to sue, until I remembered that I was broke and was therefore in no position to do anything about it.

I won the Ramp Riot four or five years in a row, so Hardcore, the skate distributors, redesigned the contest specifically to take me out. They made it a thirty-second ride on the ramp, straight off into a street course, to stop me from winning. That kind of contest has never been done, anywhere, before or since. Put it this way—there are about two dudes in the *world* that can actually ride vert and ride street, and neither of them were invited. They might as well have renamed it the "Somebody Take This Shithead's Title Away Invitational." Everyone was against me. I only had five friends, and four of them just hung out with me to drink my booze.

But I made my vert ride, and I made my street ride, and then I was like, "Fuck all of you." That was my last contest in Australia, period. All I ever did was take shit off the skate establishment over there. I always loved skating. But I stopped wanting to be around that scene. It got so that I looked forward to the contests ending so that I could get high afterward. I was done. I never lost the Ramp Riot. That was the last time I was in it.

It was hard for me to handle that skating could just be over for me as a career. I had become the king of skating in Australia and found out that made me the king of absolutely nothing. Of course, on a day-to-day basis, things could have been worse. In my mind, my life was still very awesome. Because, whatever the fuck was happening in the industry, I was arguably one of the best skaters that ever rode a vert ramp, at least in my opinion. Considering the way things were shaping up for me when I was a kid, that alone was a massive achievement.

And my life was pretty rock and roll. Sure, I drove a shitty old Chrysler Valiant that overheated all the time. The wiper fell off, and then I had to keep it in the backseat, and wipe the windshield manually when it rained. But I was still rolling around with Rachel. I would go to America as her boyfriend, and then when I came back, we would just continue the relationship like nothing had happened.

I'm sure she was fucking other people while I was gone. And I know I was. But she was this hot-ass bombshell, and guess what, everybody? She's in love with Scummy the Skateboard Rat. No, I wasn't a superstar. But to the ten dudes that gave a shit, at least, I was one lucky cunt. When I went to the ramp, I was ripping. People were in awe of what I could do. So on a day-to-day basis, I was very content. Anyway, it wasn't like I had a lot of backup career options.

As if it wasn't bad enough that vert skating was taking a shit, it was right around this time I started having to share my ramp with rollerbladers.

It's probably easy to forget how big rollerblading got for a minute there, before the world snapped to its senses. This was a very depressing time in my life. Rollerblading had become really popular all of a sudden. Snake Pit became "Snake Pit *Streetwear*." That was their cue to everyone that they now sold not just skateboards but also Rollerblades.

I should point out here that I hate rollerbladers. If you are a girl, and you want to do it to shape up your ass, fine. But there is no other reason on earth to strap on Rollerblades. I guarantee you: I will disown my children if I so much as catch them looking at Heelys.

It wasn't the rollerbladers' fault. They just had a culture that was totally different from the one I came from. In skateboarding, you can't get in our scene unless you pay your rent. And even then, you might be regarded as a kook for the rest of your life, and you never *really* get in. But rollerbladers were just so happy and cheery. They all accepted each other. They all loved each other. It was just like Christian rock—kind of similar to the real thing, except completely missing the point. They were pretending to be us with the tricks that they did. And they would try to befriend us.

Rollerblading showed up, took what was left of vert skating, and shit on it. These dudes were starting to take off, and as far as I was concerned, rollerblading was taking my money. I took it as a personal stab toward me. Street skating had already killed vert skating—rollerblading was just an extra soccer kick to the stomach, for good measure. Completely uncalled for.

It was a sad scene for me. I was skating my ramp, by myself, with dreams of somehow going back to America and getting paid. But I was stuck there, oftentimes the only skateboarder, on the worst ramp ever, surrounded by rollerbladers.

I resorted to violence. Really, what choice did I have? One day, a rollerblader dude said something to a friend of mine, Matt Anderson. The rollerblader and Matt were jawing back and forth, and I'm like, "Matt, just punch this fucking cocksucker." So now the rollerblader sets his sights on me. "You think you're so fucking tough?" he says. "Why don't you do it?"

WHAP. No hesitation. I punched him right in the nose. He went flying, skidding backward on the ground. I was the guy that never got into fights. I always avoided violence. But it was very easy for me to punch a rollerblader. That's not a human being.

This era was not the high point of my life. I even had drama with my weed dealer. He called me "Ledge," as in "Legend." He said to my dad one time, "How does it feel to have a son that's a fucking legend?" I was such a legend that I was buying weed from him on credit.

One time I wanted to settle my tab. The dealer informed me that my total was $1,600. Which was *slightly* more than I was expecting. So he's walking me through it: "You got this weed this time, and that weed that time." All well and good. "And then I made you cheese sandwiches a couple times," he said. Apparently he'd been charging me for sandwiches, when I came over to do bong rips. They weren't even good. It was Kraft singles. And his bong was this old waxed coconut. He never changed the water. The weed money was fine, but I refused to pay for these cheese sandwiches. It wasn't the money. It was the principle, damn it.

The dealer lived in a pretty shady neighborhood. He definitely knew some heavy dudes. I didn't have a house of my own, but I did have a room at my parents' house. And one time, not long after, my dad came home, and there was a robber in the place. My dad roughed him up a little bit, then told the guy to stay there while he called the cops. But the guy sprinted off. To this day, I believe that robbery was the payback.

For fucking cheese sandwiches.

Even though I was technically with Rachel this whole time, I spent a lot of those lost years in Australia having sex with as many people as humanly possible. I was out at bars all the time. And I would never shoot high. I would get to the point in a hurry—just say hi to a girl and then start making out with her. If she said no, that was a no. If she said hi back, then that meant I was going to fuck her.

Then we would go back to her house. Not so much bathrooms at the bar or anything like that. I always wanted to have sex for a long time, and try a bunch of stuff. I was really into it—playing with this, or doing that. I would bone them for as long as I possibly could, and then usually I would just be lying there. "Nope," I would decide. "Not enough." Then I would leave. Because, you know, I didn't actually *like* these women.

However awkward that first prostitute in Amsterdam might have been, apparently I got over my nerves, because very often, after the bars, whores were next on the agenda. Sometimes I would just drink so much, I was no longer even eligible to get laid. In those cases, I would go straight from the bar to St. Kilda.

St. Kilda, the shady little beach town my parents lived in when I was born, was where it was all happening, prostitute-wise. After the bars would close, or after I left some chick's house, I would go walking the streets until I found a taxi. Or if I was close enough to St. Kilda, I would walk there and find a prostitute or two. Not that I necessarily had sex with them. Ninety percent of the time it was just blow jobs in the bushes. Fifty bucks.

It became so easy. More and more, I just had an addiction to the dark side. To sin. Late at night, I would get into this mode. I knew it, too. There would be a certain drink where I already knew I'd made my decision. I was now looking for whatever drugs anybody had, and for prostitutes. And then I would sneak off. We would all be partying, and next thing you know I'd be gone.

Eventually, Rachel and me moved to St. Kilda. The grunge thing was happening in Australia at the same time it was happening in America, and St. Kilda was our Nirvana, Soundgarden, Seattle kind of place, so it was a cool place to be, in a way. Me and Rachel were living there with some musicians. A lot of my pro skateboarder friends got on heroin then. Then they all got out of skateboarding to become musicians . . . then they all became failed musicians . . . then they all just became sad piece-of-shit junkies. Grunge ruined a lot of people. At that point, I was doing as much ecstasy as I could afford. Skateboarding was the only thing that saved me from putting a needle in my arm for good. I'm a stubborn guy. In my mind, I wasn't done with skateboarding yet.

At that point, I was only friends with four or five other skaters. We all started a little team, called Flow Dog. I had always been a heavy metal guy, but these guys had more of a hip-hop vibe going on, so I started to get into that. More important, they influenced the way I skated. I was the only vert guy. Those dudes were all street skaters. But they hated everyone else, and in return, everyone else hated them. So I fit right in. I picked stuff up from them. Kickflips. Heelflips. Stuff like that.

My buddy Greg Stewart had a little video camera, and he video-taped tons of stuff. We had a video for Flow Dog. It was pretty sick, at the time, for five skaters nobody really knew. Out of all those guys, you might have known about me. But you probably would have thought of me as the "old guy." It was so weird—I was maybe twenty-three.

All my new tricks were street-oriented bullshit. If skateboarding had been that way back when I started, I wouldn't have been a skater in the first place. I'm old school. I'll take guys doing humongous 180s with style over a bunch of really technical shit. But I could hang with the new style. I invented what are known as Varial Kickflip Indies. The board flips and spins underneath your feet, at the same time. You grab the toe end of the board between your legs.

After a few years of nothingness, it started to look like vert dudes could have a career doing that stuff. I was forced to do those kinds of tricks to stay relevant in skating, so that's what I did.

And guess what?

It worked.

9.

GETTING PAID.
FINALLY.

I'd spent three years back in Australia. There was a whole new wave of skate people in America who didn't even know who I was. But now, vert skating had finally started to come back. Really, it was all due to the X Games, which started in 1995. Vert skaters weren't cool within the skateboarding world—and hadn't been for some time—but apparently ESPN and the rest of the normal world hadn't gotten the message yet.

Tas Pappas was one of the skaters that Gregor and Lee had brought along to try and beat me. That made us enemies in the beginning, but

Tas was in America now and doing pretty well and by this time we were kind of buddies. He pitched me to Element Skateboards. He said, "Ellis is as good as he used to be, plus he has all the new shit." By that, he meant all the street bullshit I had been adding to my style, thanks to skating all the time with the Flow Dog dudes.

So on my fourth six-month visa to America, I finally got paid. It wasn't much—$750 a month—but still, this was what I was waiting for. Rachel came over with me to California.

Before I left for the States, I got a personal trainer and lost a bunch of weight. I was on a mission. I went on lots of missions during my career. Sobering up. Eating right. By doing that, usually I would start doing okay in contests. Maybe I'd finish fifth at one. And I'd feel okay about myself after pulling that off, so I'd let myself start to party a little. Then maybe the next time I'd finish seventh. And I could live with that. But then, after a couple more contests, and more partying, I'd start finishing out of the top ten. Then I'd get pissed, have another epiphany about getting serious again, and I'd start another mission. But I would go off the rails again as soon as that next mission was accomplished. That was the cycle. And every mission was a little more half-assed than the one before it.

My glorious comeback in America didn't start off that great. Actually, the first big thing I did after I got on Element was go to jail. It was a DUI, in Encinitas. Pretty much bullshit. Me and Rachel had been drinking beer with Tas and his brother Ben. Not a lot. One or two. We had some weed, too, but we didn't have a lighter, so I volunteered to go get one.

Element had given me the team van, so I drove up the street to 7-Eleven. I chirped the wheels a bit when I turned the corner, and sure enough the cop was right there. He followed me into the store. He starts talking to me and makes me come out front and do all these tests. I passed them all, because I wasn't even really drunk. But then he asked me if I'd had a couple beers, and I told him yes. Because that was the way you did it in Australia. I said, "Yeah, I had a couple." Not even knowing how the game is played. And then they had me do a Breathalyzer and arrested me.

I was in jail for three days, because I was Australian and I wasn't a citizen. Rachel and Tas and Ben didn't even try to make bail. They were just drinking and smoking weed the whole time. I was far from their minds. (Obviously, when I say I was friends with Tas at that time, we weren't *that* great of friends.)

In the holding cell, I was trying to sleep, and some dude was kicking the wall right next to my head. And some big fat Mexican dude was taking the nastiest shit. There was no stall or anything. He was right there. The worst thing ever. Scared the fuck out of me. I remember trying to get my phone call, being like, *What are they doing? Why can't I get out of here?* What the cops were telling me kept changing: "You're gonna get out" one minute, and then, "No, you're *not* going to get out of here." At one point I was headed into the general population. I got the orange Vista jumpsuit and everything. Nothing happened to me in there, thank God. Nobody talked to me, and I didn't talk to them.

It was fucked up. I cried my eyes out when Rachel picked me up.

Then I went to Slam City Jam, a contest that happens every year up in Vancouver, the home of the Red Dragons. I had been friends with Sluggo going back to the Munster Cup. He gave me the thumbs-up to the rest of the Red Dragons. He introduced me to Moses Itkonen and Colin McKay, told them me and him were boys, and we all became friends. I was staying at Colin's house with Moses. Smoking weed every day. It was a great life there.

I was a legitimate fucking pro by then. I had some moves other people didn't have. I was kinda fresh. It was the last time I was ever cool. I had power, and I was going bigger than everybody. And I also had some tech shit that no one had even done yet. Heelflip Indie-to-Fakie and shit like that. Unfortunately, I blew it at Slam City Jam. I had a really good ride, and then, with fifteen seconds left, I went for an axle stall, to be safe. To make it into the finals. But my board flicked off the coping. I was already almost crying on my way back down the ramp.

I was heading back to America to try to qualify for the X Games, but I got held up at Customs. My holiday visa was for six months. It had been five and a half. They were like, "You've got two weeks left on this visa. What are you here for? What are you doing?" My story didn't match up, and they were suspicious, and threatened to deport me. I was like, "I've got money." Which was a lie. They asked me to prove it. I told them I'd go to the bank, pull it out, and show them. And they said fine: If I showed them the money, they'd let me back into the States. Otherwise, I was going home to Australia.

So I left the airport, got a taxi, and went back to downtown Vancouver. I called Moses and told him I was on the intersection of Granville and some other fucking street. He told me to stay there.

I was so stressed. Heartbroken. I thought my career was over. (As you've probably noticed by now, I thought my career was over about a thousand different times.) Moses rolled up with a doobie and a beer, told me I could keep staying at Colin's place, and said everything would be all right.

Colin had been on the Bones Brigade back when he was little, when Tony Hawk was there. Colin was like a prodigy, the future of skateboarding. He had a video part where he looked like a helmet with legs, and he did like five tricks that no one had done before. He told me I should get on Powell, the company that owns Bones

Brigade. By then, Tony Hawk was gone. Stacy Peralta—the cool part of Powell-Peralta—had left, too. But they were the only skate team at that point that had health and dental. "Take this deal," he said. "They'll never let you down." I trusted him, because he was the cool of cool in skateboarding.

After a week at Colin's house, I moved into the Red Dragons' clubhouse, where their ramp was. The guys all took their pads out of the pad room and let me stay there. I got Rachel to fly from L.A. to Vancouver. And she lived there with me, in the fucking pad room. She would shower at the gym. I would literally get hosed off outside the ramp, with my shorts on. I skated every day, until the Powell deal came through. I was basically part of the second Bones Brigade. And like most sequels, we sucked compared to the original. But Steve Caballero was still there, and he's awesome. Plus, Powell paid me two grand a month, which was so much money to me.

I lived up there for six months. That might have been the greatest time of my life. I almost just stayed there forever. A couple of things I'm kind of known for happened up in Vancouver. One is the *Whiskey* skate videos, which began around that time. I had met this snowboarder Shawn Kearns and some other Canadian guys. He was like, "You're a psycho skateboard dude? We're the psycho snowboard guys. We drink like this." And then they squeezed beers out of the can, into their mouths. They put down like eight beers each, before we even went to the bar. I drank a lot. I mean, I was the guy that would finish other people's half-empty drinks, the morning after the party. But I had never thought of it as a racing kind of thing. That's how they all rolled, though. "I'm here to drink, not to make friends." That's what they all said. And then that's what I started to say, too, before I squeezed another beer in my mouth. That kind of drinking would stimulate more and more stupid ideas in my brain—the sorts of antics that can be seen in the *Whiskey* videos. It gave me a way bigger tolerance, too. *Too* big.

Kearns and those dudes told me that Canadian bottles smash easier. So I used to smash them over my head. A lot. One time, at a party, we had two rows of bottles lined up, to have a race. Smash, smash, smash, we were off. But then I was falling behind, so I did what any real man would do—I smashed them two at a time, to catch up. The night ended with me being escorted from the premises by security, after scaling the side of this big staircase in a club, Spider-Man style.

Up in Vancouver, I also became an honorary Red Dragon. Red Dragons was started by Colin, Moses, and Sluggo, back when they were amateurs. We got the logo from the book *Red Dragon,* which came out way before the *Silence of the Lambs* movie and all that. They have the same logo on Chinese checkers—although the Chinese symbol actually stands for "center." Moses made up the little hand signal, where you throw up some fangs. We thought it was hilarious that we had a gang sign. In photos you'd see the symbol on our grip tape, or one of us throwing up the sign.

We also started calling out "Red Dragons," usually when we had just smashed something. We would break something in a hotel room, and yell, "Red Dragons." You'd say it whenever you did something badass or awesome. Here's an example of what I'm talking about:

We were street skating somewhere in Vancouver. Colin was one of two vert skaters ever who could also skate street and look like a street skater. Danny Way and Colin McKay. That's the list. Anyway, there were these policemen on mountain bikes that would bust you for fucking up ledges. It was a big deal. Every time they'd show, we'd all scatter and try to hide and the chase would be on. So Colin and Moses were skating some ledge. Those two were boring the shit out of me, as I recall, so I was just smoking some weed. The cops came up and busted us. We didn't even see them coming. They told us they were going to confiscate our boards.

Colin took his board, snapped it in half on the ground, and handed it over. "Take it," he said. "I don't give a shit. I'll get another one in five minutes. I make more money than all of you."

And then we walked off. Red Dragons.

Now it's become kind of a catchphrase on my radio show. Anybody that fucks shit up gets a Red Dragon. When I say fuck shit up, that doesn't mean kicking somebody in the face. It just means doing your thing, and not giving a shit.

Skateboarding evolves, and Red Dragons isn't the coolest thing in that world anymore. But I will always be a Red Dragon. Me and all the other guys have big-ass tattoos, from our armpits down to our waists. I was the first guy to get it. I took becoming a Red Dragon very serious, because I had a lot of respect for them. And I think, because of the respect I showed them for making me a Red Dragon, it made me even more of a real Red Dragon. "Just so you know, you're the first Red Dragon that isn't from Canada," they told me. "So it's a big deal." We were almost whispering. "I know. I realize this. And I appreciate it. Thank you." No ceremony or anything, but it was serious. It was always very serious to me.

WHILE I WAS STAYING IN Vancouver, I made my triumphant return to Amsterdam, on another European skate tour. I had been to Amsterdam twice by now. Rachel didn't come with me, because I would have had to pay her way the whole time, and I couldn't afford it. Anyway, I didn't really need her around for the kinds of things I tended to do in Amsterdam.

The first time I was in Amsterdam I only had the one hooker, and I was really scared. But that unleashed the beast. So the next time I was there, I was high the whole time and I was getting a *lot* of prostitutes. By this trip—the third one—I had a good solid drinking problem, plus a high level of ecstasy use. I remember asking people for ecstasy in Amsterdam, which you don't do. They didn't actually have ecstasy there; they just gave you a dried piece of dog turd, or some other heinous ecstasy substitute. I also reached new heights as far as prostitutes were concerned. There was a street full of them, and I would just go from one to the next. It was like a candy store to me.

While I was in the middle of a particularly epic run, word started to travel. "Ellis is working his way down the street, one hooker at a time. This guy is on fire!" Fellow skaters were showing each other all the doors I had already gone in and out of. My T-shirt's all sweaty and stuff. I'm working it out. I'm going for it. I remember coming out of one, and a bunch of people had stopped to wait for me. Eventually there were fifty or sixty pro skateboarders cheering me on. Guys were giving me money, to see how far I would go. All of mine was already gone. It was like, "Here's another fifty, Ellis. Now go knock on *that* door." And off I go. Every door I come back out of, there's a crowd of people cheering for me. I visited five or six girls on that street alone. Looking back, I don't even know how that's possible. But it happened. I was there.

I was thoroughly invigorated, until I noticed one skater's wife standing there. They were a nice couple. Well, I thought they were. It turns out their major hobby was taking art photos of his dick, and stuff like that. But at the time, I didn't know that these were two of the most twisted individuals in skateboarding. Then, my only thought was, *Aw man, this is somebody's wife. How embarrassing.* With the boys, it's all right. But I don't want somebody's wife to know. I kind of apologized. But then she said, "I think it's cool. It shows you have a lot of stamina." I thought that was a bit odd. I remember wondering, *Does that mean you want some as well?*

Late that night, a Swedish professional skateboarder I knew was around. I thought he was a nerd, and I didn't like him, because, you know, he was Swedish. I caught him at three o'clock in the morning, convincing a hooker to have sex with him for $12.50. I waited outside, until he came out, and I was like, "Dude, did you just pay $12.50 for that?" And in his Swedish accent he said, "Dood, you can bah-gain. It is not ull-ways fifty doll-uhs." This was amazing news. So then off I went, on my magical journeys with this creepy Swedish man, trying to get people to jack me off for five bucks.

That's how I learned that you can indeed negotiate the price you pay for hookers. I recall doing a bit of bargaining with a prostitute I met later on in Amsterdam. By this point in the trip, I'd been drinking for two days. I was not at my sharpest. She was this really hot black chick . . . only, as it turned out, she wasn't really a chick. Look, if I really knew it was dude, I'd be the first to tell you, especially if it sold more books. But to look at her, she was a girl. Even when he bent me over, I still thought, *Wow, cool, here comes some weird, next-level shit.* I'm thinking it's something kinky, a reach-around of some sort.

And then I felt something on my ass. *In* my ass. Somewhere between the two. Dick and ass definitely made contact. I remember thinking, *Well, good luck with that.* Because I don't like things near my ass. I think I had already tried to stick a knife handle in my ass when I was a kid, and that was not an experience that I had enjoyed. And now this prostitute is grabbing my hips and trying to push something in. That's when it really began to dawn on me. He had both his hands on my hips. That pretty much ruled out a hand job.

I'm happy to say that my politeness kicked in. I might have said, "Oh, fuck! A dick!" But I've never been a person that got angry at gay people, or about homosexuality. I basically apologized. "Oh! I'm sorry! That wasn't what I was expecting. It's cool that you want to do that to me and all. It's just not what I was looking for, thank you." I let him keep the money, and off I went, pretending that it didn't even happen.

Until I went back to Vancouver and told Rachel that I'd had sexual relations with a man. This involved admitting that I cheated on her, although of course I left out the other fifty prostitutes. I remember crying, and her consoling me, saying everything was going to be okay, with me being all like "I think I'm gay!" She felt sorry for me, so I didn't get in trouble.

Later on, knowing that having things stuck in my ass was something I was not fond of, Rachel jammed a finger in there while I was having sex with another woman. That was yet another confirmation that I do not enjoy receiving anal. Because that was the first time I ever contemplated punching a girl in the head. I remember pulling out, turning around, and saying, "Don't ever do that again. I'm going home."

This happened during a foursome with another skater. He had brought over a hooker. Or a stripper. Same difference. We used to have foursomes a lot. Trading girls. Me and him never did things with each other, but we switched girls, in the same room. Which is borderline gay as well. When Rachel was finished with him, I was still at it with his chick, so my girlfriend dealt with her feelings over that situation by shoving a finger in my ass. And I put my pants on and left.

This is around when Rachel became a stripper. After I got on the Bones Brigade, I was on a six-year work visa, so I could go home whenever I wanted. I went back to Australia at least once a year, for a couple months at a time. She usually traveled with me, although sometimes she might stay behind at home when I left. We were in Australia together when she decided that she wanted to dance. She wanted to make some money.

I went with her to the Gentleman's Club in Melbourne, which is the best strip club in Australia. I waited outside while she was auditioning. At first I was on board with the plan, but by the time she came out, I remember saying, "I've got a bad feeling about this. I don't think we should do this." She was like, "Yeah, maybe you're right." And then she started working there. She was modeling for a nude magazine a year after that.

For a while at least, this setup was *incredibly* awesome. She would make like six hundred bucks a night. She would bring it back, in cash, and we would go out and drink and take ecstasy. Between my paychecks and her paychecks we could do whatever we wanted. The cycle just kept going, every night.

I would go to the strip club with her. That was how I spent a lot of my afternoons. She would get money and give it to me, and then I would give it to someone else, to dance for me. Tons of times there were arguments. She was crazy, and so was I. We drank too much, and we were both whores, so we drove each other up the wall, constantly.

My dad used to see this girl who was a stripper at the same place where Rachel danced. His chick was the same age as Rachel. On the nights his girlfriend was off, him and her would go in the club and get dances together.

Speaking of my dad: by this point—my midtwenties—I thought it might have registered with him that I had a bit of a legitimate thing going on with the whole skateboarding racket. But apparently I was wrong.

Dad had moved into another house, and I'd come back and stay there when I was home. I was happy to finally be in America for real, but I did get homesick. Plus I liked to come back and show off a bit. I had a little money, and a bunch of new sneakers and clothes and shit.

Dad and Marn had a spare room. It had a little bed. A check came in the mail from the Bones Brigade. And my father was, like, "What's this?" I was like, "What the fuck does it look like? It's a check."

"From skateboarding?"

Really? "Yeah, dude."

"Do they come all the time?"

"Yes. Every month, I get that. All the time. And other ones, from all my other sponsors."

And he was like, "Jay. You should take this shit serious."

"What the fuck are you talking about? Who the fuck do you think paid for my plane ticket to get here? What did you think I was doing?"

"I dunno. Selling a bit of weed or something?"

This *had* to be a joke. He *had* to know that I was a pro skateboarder. I was internationally known in the skate community. I had traveled the world. Skate videos. Magazines. Fuck, I'd had sponsors for ten years. He *had* to be fucking with me. But with my dad, who knows?

BY THIS TIME, AS A skater, I was as good as anybody. I'm not saying I could have been Tony Hawk. But I could have had my run. Beat everyone, crush, take no prisoners, for like a year straight. Skateboarding never had to end, unless I wanted it to. Unfortunately, my skills as a party guy were also on a pretty elite level. For the first time in my life, I was making a little money, and I dove into all the opportunities the lifestyle had to offer.

When I was back in Australia, things would get particularly ugly. People had jobs. I was literally the only pro skater in Australia. I was the only person that didn't have to get up in the morning. So when the party ended on Saturday, well, it didn't end for me. I didn't make a *lot* of money, but I lived at my parents' house. And my girlfriend was a stripper. I was consuming pretty epic amounts of booze and weed. People were blown away by what I was doing, like, "Are you okay, dude?" And I had no idea what they were talking about. I honestly didn't realize it was all that much.

I started to figure that out because when I would bring girls home and smoke weed with them, almost all of them would vomit. And then they would pass out for the night. I couldn't put it together. I would have a bunch of drinks, and then go out, and then bring some chick back. And then I'd give her a couple of *my* drinks, which is a glass of vodka with some ice in it, which I called a vodka tonic. And then we'd rip into a couple of blunts, which were half weed, half tobacco. I called those Mull-Bongs (because you mixed the weed and tobacco up, into a mulch). And then the girl would usually go to the bathroom and vomit for an hour, and I'd just be there smoking blunts and playing video games, like, *What the fuck's her problem?*

Meanwhile, cocaine started to become a thing in America. Coke is crazy expensive in Australia. And it's garbage. Not worth the trouble. Every time I would go back to the States, as soon as I got off the plane, I would go to Carlsbad and meet a guy. We'd snap some Mull-Bongs and get some bumps. I loved California. But I remember thinking that sometimes, coming back, I was more excited about doing coke than about being back in California to skate.

Cocaine began for me when I lived with this crazy hippie guy who was a dealer. A bunch of skateboard dudes I knew lived in his house, and I needed a place to stay. That's how I got introduced to him. It wasn't like a straight-up crack house or anything—I was the only one of us who used to buy coke off the guy. Like a lot of things I try, once I got it, I got really into it. Fast. You had to watch me around it. There would never be any left by the time I went to sleep. The hippie guy had some crazy whore girlfriend who was superold. She would do so much coke that, for some reason, she had to have her mouth open and her tongue out. She would just be like that, in the corner of the room, all the time. Panting, because she was so high.

I would always get blow off this dude. I just remember sitting there, many a night, with my bourbon, and my Discman. Or I would play guitar, with my amp plugged into my headphones. Rachel could never do as much coke as me, so even when she was in the States with me, I would just be hanging out in this guy's house by myself, drinking, smoking cigarettes, smoking weed, trying to make the cocaine wear off so I could do some more. Until one time, he was like, "You're not looking so good. I'm gonna have to cut you off." And this dude was fucked beyond belief. For him to call that on me was saying something.

After Rachel had been dancing for a while in Australia, we got a place together in Hollywood, and she started dancing over in the States. That was the worst part of our relationship. No other skateboarders live in Hollywood. I had to drive to Ventura to skate, like an hour away. We were there so Rachel could dance. So we could have more money. That's when we found a guy who introduced us to crystal meth. We would snort crystal meth, and she would dance, and that's when we both met Lemmy from Motörhead.

I had told Rachel that if anybody famous ever came into the strip club, she should bring them home to meet me. Don't ask me why. But one time, I was in the apartment, and she was in the elevator, and she buzzed up to inform me that she was with "Lenny from Motorbreath." I'm like, "Do you mean Lemmy from Motörhead?" "Yeah, yeah," she said. "Just hit the button."

So I let her in, along with good ol' "Lenny from Motorbreath," who sat down and started snorting crystal out of a bag. I could tell he thought I didn't notice that he was taking drugs in front of us. Rachel had a little skirt on and pink panties, and he was just relentlessly staring at her underwear. He played my Gibson Explorer guitar and told me about how Metallica had all come to his birthday party dressed as him. But it got to the point where Lemmy was no longer listening to anything that anybody said. He was just focused on my girlfriend's crotch. He definitely thought we were gonna have a threesome. I gather he would not have minded double-teaming my girlfriend with my assistance, if that was the way it had to be. Finally I had to pull that whole "Well, it's getting late" routine to get him to leave.

By the time the third or fourth X Games came around, I couldn't even manage to qualify. I was so shitfaced. I was living in Hollywood, doing crystal with Rachel. Drinking all day, every day. Not sleeping for days at a time. Waddling around thinking no one knew my secret life. I was always selling a story about how everything was gonna work out. Trying to sell it to myself. Telling myself this life I led was indeed very awesome.

And let's face it, it was a *little* bit awesome: I lived in Hollywood with a stripper. I could get threesomes. I was a pro skater. I didn't have a real job. I could afford to buy a bunch of drugs and booze.

But then Rachel would wake me up in the middle of the night, saying, "I'm going to get weed." I'm like, "You can't get weed. It's four in the morning. It's fucking Hollywood. Someone will stab you." So I'd have to go out with her. Steve Gourlay, my old Flow Dog teammate, used to think I talked too mean to Rachel. But then he came over from Australia, stayed at my house for two days, and was like, "You need to get her the fuck out of here. She is a fucking psychopath." His opinion completely changed. I was no longer the bad guy. I remember one time waking up, and she had some crazy techno music on. She was eating rice with Jack Daniel's in it. I remember thinking, *Fucking hell, Rachel. You're fucking up.*

I suppose you could have said the same about me. One time I hired a very enterprising hooker who grabbed a lightbulb from the bathroom in our hotel room so we could smoke crystal out of it. (I smoked crack out of a lightbulb with some other chick, later. Lightbulbs were used as paraphernalia several times along the way.) Smoking the crystal, I remember being especially high. I vomited while having sex. The hooker got pretty weird at that point, but I stayed focused and powered through. It was only a couple days later that I realized it had been the midsex vomiting where I lost her. After she took off, I manipulated my penis for like two days, until it looked like a deformed mushroom. My foreskin was so swollen I couldn't even piss.

My antics were definitely an issue to the Bones Brigade, although in the end I lasted on that team for like ten years. I was on the Bones Brigade when I got one of my most gruesome injuries ever—my wrist again. I was riding in a contest when I suddenly woke up in the flat with my wrist doing this weird S-bend thing. I grabbed it, and tried to shake it back into place, but it wouldn't work. I was on my way to doing really well in this contest. I was gonna win. So I wouldn't let the medic take me away.

I got some duct tape and taped my wrist together, and then I tried to skate in the contest again. But halfway through my ride, my wrist flexed, and it all crunched, so then I got my team manager to take me to the hospital. They did x-rays, and they thought it was dislocated. They put these sock things on my fingers, like the suit they put on you to protect you from a shark bite. And then they put a weight on my elbow, and they started pulling on it, to try to pop it back in. I was on morphine by this point, so it wasn't as bad as it sounds. But then the nurse came in with the x-rays and revealed that my wrist wasn't dislocated—it was crushed. It had done a full 180. It was upside down, against my hand. Oh, and all the bones in my hand were broken, too. And they had therefore been yanking on this thoroughly mangled area of my body for absolutely no reason.

It was too crazy of a surgery for them to do. So they put a half-cast on it and sent me on my way with a prescription for painkillers. And then, because my team manager was such a pussy, he wouldn't let me get my painkillers unless I stayed in the hotel. But I wanted to go out that night and party. So I went out and drank, because I was already on morphine, and when I drank, there was even less pain.

I woke up in the morning in some chick's hotel room, in the most amazing pain imaginable, threatening this poor woman to get in a car and drive me to my hotel—NOW!—so that I could find my shitty team manager to give me my fucking pain pills before I pulled my own eyeballs out.

At one point, everyone on the Bones Brigade agreed to kick me off. But right before the intervention went down, I got Mike Vallely's back in an epic fight at Wembley Stadium in London, and not by choice. I was on a ramp when someone came up to me and said, "Your boy's in trouble," and I ran over in time to help Mike—who was with his wife and daughter at that particular moment—fend off several English hooligan types. Mike was the head of the Bones Brigade, so he ended up overruling everybody and I stayed on the team.

Although you couldn't have blamed them if they had gotten rid of me. Another time, back in Australia on the Warped Tour, I had to get lost in a hurry after I rammed a security guy's car with a garbage can. (That was an accident. Not the ramming the car part. The part about doing it to security.) I managed to make it back to the tent I was sleeping in, and I had to piss, but I was so drunk, I fell over. I was also so drunk I couldn't get up. And I was *also* so drunk I couldn't stop pissing. So I pissed all over myself. And then I passed out. When I woke up, my hand was underwater. My phone was right next to my hand, also underwater. This was a waterproof tent. It was not water. It was my own urine.

I hadn't made it all the way in the tent—my feet were hanging out. Steve Caballero saw me on his way to the shower. Bear in mind, Steve Caballero was on the Bones Brigade when I started skating. Steve Caballero is *still* on the Bones Brigade. He later told me there was a colony of ants trooping over my feet, heading toward whatever food was inside there with me. My feet were so burned they were blistering. Even on the bottoms. Meanwhile, inside the tent, the heat was turning the urine into steam, creating a sort of piss sauna in which I'd been sleeping.

I was up and walking around by the time Steve was done with his shower. I love that guy. I just nodded at him. "What's up, Stevie."

Nowadays, when he tells that story, Steve will tell you he was amused. But at the time, he was not happy.

Whatever. I still skated all the demos that day.

PART THREE

10.

OUT WITH THE OLD BITCH,

AND IN WITH THE NEW

For Rachel and me, cheating on each other was always secret. That is, until we agreed to try an open relationship. I was gonna fuck some chick, and she was gonna fuck this other guy. I had sex with mine and came back, and then she went with her dude. I remember waiting out the front of the house we were staying in. I was waiting, waiting, waiting. She was supposed to come back at midnight, but she didn't come home until like three in the morning. I was still out front. He dropped her off, and I was like, "So'd you fuck him?" She said no. "So you just hung out, until three o'clock in the morning?" She said yeah. I'm like, "Well, what the fuck is that? What, do you *like* him or something?"

That was the beginning of the end. That guy ended up being her boyfriend, secretly. There was this whole fucking drama. It went on for a long time. All these people that knew him wanted to beat me up. He was a thug kind of guy, so he could arrange to make that kind of stuff happen. Strippers—friends of Rachel's—would be vibing me, telling me I needed to get out of the club. I was like, "I was here first! Who the fuck are you?"

I remember coming back from America, one of the times when Rachel had stayed behind in Australia. I got us a hotel in St. Kilda, and we were in the Jacuzzi having sex, and Rachel started crying. "What's wrong?" I said. "I'm back. Everything will be fine." And then I found out. She told me a couple days later. She was crying because she was cheating on the boyfriend that she loved.

Which was not me, apparently.

Still, we were off and on, off and on, for a long time after. For some reason, I insisted on torturing myself. I went to America again, and I came back with an engagement ring. Like, maybe a thousand bucks? That was a lot of money for me. Fucking idiot. I went to Chapel Street, in Prahran, one town over from St. Kilda, and I saw them. I knew his bike. I knew everything about him. I saw him ride by, with her on the back. I took the ring and just threw it. Up in the air, over this store behind me. Well, there goes that. I went to a 7-Eleven, and they had a life-sized cardboard cutout of Rachel. It was an advertisement for some kind of soda, I think. She modeled for it. It was like I couldn't get away from her.

I was obsessed with that dude for a long time. It tore me up that she left me to be with him.

This was when I truly became abusive with alcohol. I always

drank and partied. But during this time—when I would keep breaking up and making up with her—that's when I built the tolerance that I would later pay the price for. I remember drinking myself to sleep. Waking up with a bottle of vodka in my hand that I hadn't finished. I would be passed out, sitting up against the wall, and I would pick up right where I left off. I learned how to ignore a hangover, and just drink through it. I kept drinking, and my tolerance became higher, and I could just consume massive amounts of alcohol at any time.

There was this anger when I would drink. Not toward anybody else; toward myself. I was angry that I had let her go. That I was losing her to this other guy. I remember the pain of drinking, of swallowing. Making faces as it went down. That pain would make me angrier, and then that anger was the fuel to drink more.

In America I was kind of okay. Out of sight, out of mind. But every time I came back to Australia, my heart would be broken all over again. Everyone I knew had a job to go to every day, except me. I spent a lot of time by myself. I would drink in alleyways and parks. I would buy beer and go to a park and just sit there and envision a better life. Rachel loving me again. Me being in charge of things. Big time. A success. Her new guy fucking dying. Me being the greatest skateboarder ever. Being rich. Having cars. Going to restaurants and fancy hotels. Having people love me, so that she could see it. I knew that was what all these fantasies were about. If I became a massive big deal, I could get back at her. Or get back together with her. Fuck, *both*. At the time I probably would have told you revenge was the priority, but really I just wanted to be back together with her so that she could ruin my life yet again.

Easily, she was the person that broke my heart. Easily. For all the cheating and bullshit, Rachel and me had been a serious, long-term thing. I really thought I was going to marry her. I thought we would have kids. I'd been in a relationship with Rachel for seven or eight years.

But the two of us weren't completely finished until me and Sara got together.

This must have been 1997. I had known Sara for a while. Her and Rachel were like sisters. Like twins. Guys used to pay extra for the two of them to dance together at the club where they worked. A couple of times Sara had come with Rachel to a New Year's party we used to have at my parents' vacation house in Tanjil.

The last time Rachel came to that party, Sara was with her again, and by the time they showed up, I'd already been out by the pool, puking my ass off from the amount of alcohol I'd consumed by lunchtime. Because it was New Year's, you know? Getting ready for the big night. Sara gave me like four ecstasies, to fight the alcohol poisoning. So by the time it was dark, I was back up and running, and still guzzling booze.

Sara was amazingly attractive. Hotter than Rachel. She had this crazy ass. Very tempting. I'm not going to lie and say the thought hadn't crossed my mind. That night, I remember spending hours out in front of the house with her. I was balancing her, with my feet on her stomach, holding her hands. Holding her up in the air. It wasn't hard to see where this was going. Fucking inevitable shit.

And then one night I slept in that little bed at my parents' house, with Rachel and Sara on either side. And in the middle of the night I made out with Sara. But when I woke up, I thought it was a dream. Later on, Rachel had to go somewhere, and Sara brought it up at lunch. I told her I had dreamed that I made out with her. "So did I!" she told me. Well, imagine that.

That same night, Sara drove me and my friends out to a bar, where I proceeded to have sex with the ugliest, fattest girl on the planet. My friends tried to stop me. It was like two o'clock in the morning. "I'm getting laid. Fuck you guys." She was so disgusting. I remember thinking I should have just got a hooker. But later on in our relationship, Sara told me that that night she had wanted me to stay in her car with her. She was going to fuck me.

I remember the moment it hit me. We went to her hairdresser— actually, we had the *same* hairdresser—and I remember sitting next to Sara, thinking, *This is the hottest chick ever. I am in love with her.*

We had sex, and fell in love, instantly, while having sex. Within three days I wanted to marry her. I think I might have even asked her within a week. She said yes, and then she told me all this shit about Rachel fucking that other dude on the side. The whole time. And yes, I totally believe that Rachel was cheating on me the entire time we were together. Like I've said, we were exactly the same. Whatever I was doing, I guarantee you she was doing all the same exact shit. Maybe a tiny bit less, because I'm a dude, but still.

After I started going out with Sara, the news got back to Rachel through someone else. Up until then, Rachel seemed to almost enjoy staying in my life and making me miserable. But now, she didn't do anything. There was a reason for that, as it turns out. I didn't know it at the time, but Rachel did: Sara was crazy, and Sara would fucking kill you. Sara became Rachel's enemy. And Sara hated the dude that was fucking Rachel, too. She would talk shit about him to me. Which made me love her even more.

There was another reason Rachel and her dude cut out of our lives so quick: Sara's mum was tied in heavy with a bunch of gangsters. She was friends with an Aussie living legend called Chopper Read.

Chopper Read is a man who could not read or write, who would shoot people during crystal meth deals, and go to clubs and cap people. Shit like that. He went to jail and fucked with people there to the point where they were going to kill him. So, making a power move, Chopper got another person to chop his ears off so that he would be moved to safety in another part of the prison. When he finally got out of jail, he started killing bad people. He claimed the police had hired him to do it—which the police have denied. Then he went back to prison and wrote a book, which became the number-one-selling book in Australia. He was on *60 Minutes* in Australia, in jail, saying, "I got the number one book, and I can't fucking read, mate. So who's laughing now?" Chopper Read is gnarly. They made a movie about him.

Chopper wasn't the only heavy dude that Sara's mum was friends with. He was just the most famous. Rachel's new dude might have been a bit of a thug, but nowhere near the level of some of Sara's mum's friends. Maybe Chopper Read himself wasn't going to go kill Rachel's boyfriend, but her boyfriend knew some of Sara's mum's other friends and these were not people to be fucked with. Not on account of me, anyway. Rachel's dude had had people rough me up in clubs a couple times. Stuff like that. But now, because Sara was in the picture, Rachel's boyfriend wouldn't do anything to me anymore, or to Sara. We weren't worth the trouble. I was in my late twenties. And all of a sudden, I was in the clear.

I really didn't care about Rachel anymore. I had the hottest chick, and we were in love. Sara was way smarter than Rachel. Way more organized. She had an apartment that was clean. She loved to have things stacked in the fridge correctly. Meanwhile, Rachel was rice and bourbon.

I WAS STANDING OUTSIDE A castle when it hit me that the wedding was a bad idea. That's right—I married Rachel's best friend, who looked exactly like her. Just like my dad left my mum for *her* best friend. Like father like son, I guess.

I was dressed in a suit, with my brothers and my best man. My dad was there. You know how people talk about cold feet? Well, right before I walked into this castle, into my wedding, reality started to sink in hard. This was really gonna go down. I was like, *Man, I'm really gonna get married to this person?* We barely even knew each other. It happened so quick. My big memory of the night was my friends getting wasted and doing acid and scaling the castle walls, and me missing out on the fun because I had just gotten married and had to stay with Sara. From what I hear, everybody had a great time.

I don't know if I was in love with her. I know I *thought* I was. We would *say* we loved each other all the time. And I really did enjoy being around her. Sure, I loved her, I guess. I knew deep down that it wasn't gonna work. But I've always been a fan of just going for it and seeing what happens.

So within a year of breaking up with Rachel, I was married to Sara. I lived in her apartment for a while. She had tons of money from stripping. And as far as I was concerned, skateboarding was just about done. I'd had my run as a pro, but there wasn't gonna be another act for me in America. And Australia didn't give a shit about what I'd done. Being the best dude there never did anything for me in any way. There were people in Australia who were millionaires off the skateboarding industry. I was the best guy for years, and I was still setting up skateboards and selling them at some shop so I could get money for weed. I could go in street contests, as a vert skater, and still win, because I was that good. But I was broke.

I had taken some shitty sponsors, to keep some money coming in. Instead of riding for the best guy for low money, I'd ride for shit guys for bigger cash. I barely skated. When I did, it was usually only to shoot an ad. I made Sara wear a bikini and stand on a vert ramp. I did a Nosegrind on a bar she was holding above her head, for a double-page ad. The photo was from the back, so you could focus properly on her ass. For a white girl, she had a pretty big ass.

Don't get me wrong—if you didn't know any better, you would think my life was still very awesome. Sara made a bunch of money from stripping, and I still had skateboard checks coming in. I was still on the Bones Brigade. We moved into a house in Highett, close to where I grew up in Sandringham. I always had new sneakers, and a cool haircut. I drove a 4Runner. I didn't know anyone else who had one of those, much less a skateboarder.

But there was no second career on the way for me. What the hell could I ever do, other than skate? I said it all the time. What—was I gonna start a T-shirt company? I can't spell. I can't add. I'm not the sharpest guy, but I do know that if you can't spell, and you can't add, odds are your T-shirt company isn't going to do that well. No one was going to partner up with me. I tried being a rep for Innes skate decks. I went to stores with another guy who knew what he was doing, driving around Victoria, trying to get preorders. They would order shirts for other skaters, but they would tell me to my face that they didn't want the Jason Ellis shirt.

I thought that being with a stripper might be my best chance to have some money and an okay life. Plus, when I met Sara, she was into a lot of the same crazy stuff that I was, when it came to partying and sex. But then, all of a sudden, she just changed and wasn't into any of it. The more serious we became, the more she encouraged me to sober up. With force. She was in charge of our relationship. That usually is the case when you go out with me. I just let everybody run my life. If I get to make the call on a few things here and there, I'm happy. But Sara was molding me into something. Trying to, anyway. And she wasn't going to give up, either. She was very determined to get her way.

I really did try to make an effort. But I was still really wasted, and obviously I was nowhere near ready to quit. I rebelled, even more. I took drugs more aggressively. For different reasons. I just didn't want to be me anymore. Despite Sara's attempts to change me, I not only stayed wasted a lot of the time, I managed to pick up and maintain a heroin habit for a year. She somehow never caught on. It wasn't an all-the-time thing, but it happened often enough. I made a full video part for Powell, chasing the dragon in between takes.

I would be out drinking. And then I would start to feel that vibe again. That sneaky feeling, like I've got to go off on my own and take this party to the next level, and I don't want anybody around.

Cash in hand, I would head over to St. Kilda, looking for hookers. My goal at this point was to get a blow job and get some heroin. And then I would chase the dragon. I had my foil, and my pen. I had learned that from a pro skateboarder friend, this one night up in Vancouver. The guy talked me into trying black tar heroin, and it was a really fun time. We were all laughing, and at the end of the night, I wound up with two chicks. It was a bit of information I never forgot: put the heroin on the foil, heat it, and smoke it through the pen. Easy.

So now, late night in St. Kilda, I would find some hookers. There were only a couple of streets where they all hung out, so it wasn't hard to find them. They would get me the heroin—I never once dealt with a heroin dealer directly—and I would buy them some heroin, too. And they would suck my dick, and I would give them the money for that and for the drugs. Then I would take the heroin and drive back down to Sandringham, where I used to hang out by the beach. There's these parking lots with loads of trees, sort of in the woods. You can walk off down to the ocean. I used to hang out there when I was a kid. I know the area from when I used to be on foot, before I had a car. So I knew I could trust being there and not get caught. I knew the side streets to get in and out of there. Shitfaced. I'm on heroin, wasted out of my mind, at four o'clock in the morning. But I'm driving down streets where I know there's no po-po. There's no crime in Sandringham. So I would take it down there. I remember thinking the heroin was no big deal. Just something I did when I was drunk. I only took a little bit.

But then this one night, before I even left the bar, I made the decision that I was going to smoke way more than I had ever smoked before. I had drunk a lot that day. So I got the heroin. I had a good fucking chunk of it this time. Before that, I would maybe feel a little numb or something from it. But this time, I was *high*. I remember heating it up, sucking it in, and thinking, in a split second, *Oh. Okay. That's what everybody's been going on about.* I was vomiting for like an hour. And thinking, *Man, I can't believe I've come this far. To be here. Back in Sandringham, vomiting on heroin.* I never thought I'd be that guy. I had never done heroin in the past, because I had had such a bad opinion of it.

That realization was so sad to me, but I just didn't care anymore. And so that was my routine. Hookers and heroin. Not too long after that, I'm out there again in St. Kilda. And a lot of hookers think I'm a cop, because they're all so sketchy and out of their balls. But I finally convince these two chicks. I had to buy so much heroin to convince them, because I wanted them both. At this point, I was just trying to think of more and more creepy things that I could do.

They take me back to this place, about a hundred yards from the hotel where Rachel had cried while we had sex in a Jacuzzi. This spot kind of reminded me of a movie, where cops are chasing a guy in, like, Chinatown, and they're following him through all these weird back rooms. You know, one room leads to a restaurant, and another one leads to a bookstore, maybe, and so on. I have no fucking idea where I am. I've gone upstairs, downstairs, through random doors, seen random dudes, you name it.

And we get to this little room. The hookers are so smacked out, they inform me that there is no way we're snorting or smoking anything. These chicks were hard-core. They were there to shoot it up. And so I'm like, "Well, can you give me some?" I remember figuring that these two were so cracked out, there was no way I was gonna OD, because they were going to give me the smallest amount possible and keep the rest for themselves.

It was a new needle. I asked about that. At that moment, I actually wasn't even worried about AIDS. I was just worried about becoming a junkie, now that I was about to shoot up. Although obviously at that point I wasn't all that worried about anything. I had just given up completely. When I look back on it, that point was the lowest time in my life. I didn't know it at the time. But for me to even be cool with that—I don't even know that person. I don't understand why I would do that.

So they shot me up, and then I started fucking one of them. I don't even know if I fucked both of them. I can't remember. Then the next thing I do remember, my pants are on and they're holding my hand and they're leading me somewhere. I barely even know what's happening. And then I'm alone.

The cold wakes me up. I'm shivering, and wondering where I am. I'm in a park. In St. Kilda. It's three, maybe four in the morning. It's not Compton, but for Melbourne, this is the most ghetto area imaginable. And it's where everybody does heroin. My first thought is to get the fuck out of there. And then I start thinking things through a bit. Why did they drop me off? I vomited a bit and started to stagger away. As my brain started to come to, it hit me. Oh my God!

I reached for my wallet. They robbed me. While I was fucking one of them, the other one got me. I had a lot of cash in those days. I remember thinking, *Right. Don't do heroin. Ever again.* I don't think I did, either. That was the last time. That's what happens when you do heroin with hookers: they steal your life savings. Which, at that particular moment in time, for me, was eight hundred dollars.

IT WAS DURING THE HEIGHT of my heroin adventures that the X Games came calling.

X Games had been around for a while at this point. But when the energy drinks showed up, it got way bigger.

There was this dude who worked at ESPN, and he got my number in Australia. He called me and said that he wanted me to come over to America to work for them. I think one time, at a Vans Triple Crown in Huntington Beach, people in skateboarding had gotten the idea that maybe I could be an announcer. The real announcer was stuck in the bathroom or something. Probably sick, or gakked out of their mind. So I picked up the mike and started ripping into everyone there. I got the whole crowd laughing pretty good, just pulling jokes out of my ass.

I reminded the ESPN guy that I lived in Australia. He didn't see that as a problem. He named a dollar figure. It was more than I'd ever been paid for skateboarding. He asked if I had an agent. I said no. He said, "Good, you don't need one." That sounded a bit odd. I had a skate friend who had an agent named Steve Astephen, so I asked Steve if that sounded cool to him. He said that no, that did *not* sound cool. But Steve knew the ESPN guy, as it turned out, so Steve talked to him. And then, I had an agent, I got flown to America, and ESPN paid me.

Just like that, I was back. Fuck, I was better than back. In skateboarding, TV time is all the sponsors care about. Usually the top three guys get on TV, if they're lucky. Well, guess what? So does the guy who's announcing. I wasn't gonna get top three, because I was shitfaced and blowing it by then. I wasn't terrible at skateboarding—I could still hang—but announcing was a sure thing.

I remember getting a six-thousand-dollar-a-month retainer from ESPN. Every month—not just for the X Games. They had these other contests—B3 and so on—and they wanted me on the road announcing all of them.

This was *very* awesome. Things had fucking changed.

BALLIN'

I jumped at the chance to work for ESPN. They were throwing me a lifeline I desperately needed. In 2000, I left Sara behind in Australia just to make sure the job was going to work out. Things were pretty rocky with us anyway. So I was solo when I moved back to California, for a little while anyway. Things were looking up. I was back in America. I was getting paid by ESPN. My agent, Steve, was moronic enough to cosign a car lease with me—a $900-a-month BMW 740iL. I bought a pug, Grimey. He was my boy. He came everywhere with me. I was the first kook to walk around with a little fucking dog and a fancy car. I was riding around in do-rags, wearing stupid shit and gold chains, and I had my little pug with me. I was like the Paris Hilton of skateboarding, before Paris Hilton even existed.

Most of my life was just announcing. Which was dangerous for a guy like me, because if I'm announcing, then I don't have to be sober for anything. I would show up just stinking. I remember at a contest in Texas or somewhere, I got into an argument with some guy. He had a Bones Brigade T-shirt on, but he was a rollerblader. I ripped his T-shirt off him as he went past me, and then just walked off. The dude punched me in the head. Kind of beat me up, really. I couldn't get off the ground. I was so drunk. I remember I got up and then fell back down, while looking up at him. *Oh my God,* I'm thinking. *This is really happening.* I got beat up good. By a rollerblader.

I started hanging out tons with Colin McKay. Colin drank and partied, although nothing close to how I did. Colin loved this life that I was suddenly living. Now, Colin has his dog, Reggie, riding around with him in his Mercedes, because I made that look glamorous. He glorified the image I was pushing to the point where it influenced me to go even harder.

I went to some awards show—the ESPYs, I think—with Colin in 2001. We were hanging out, and I was doing some bumps of cocaine, and somebody was giving me free jewelry to wear for the night. Some obscenely stupid shit. I just grabbed whatever they would let me have. I had a do-rag on, and a fucking gold Rocawear shirt, and this gold chain with a diamond cross, and bracelets. At this point, I knew I was a fucking clown, but I was embracing it. I had it figured out, at least in my mind. I would tell people, "I'm not white, I'm Australian."

And then one of the hosts for the red carpet didn't show up. Although it wasn't a red carpet. It was the green carpet, because, as you may have heard, ESPN is *extreme.* So somebody asked me, "Do you want to do interviews on the green carpet?" They said they would pay me. So I said sure, what do I care? A girl who worked for ESPN kept openly handing me vodka and cranberries. It was an accepted part of my image that from time to time I would be this crazy wasted guy. So she was feeding the monster. Because if the monster didn't get more beverages, he would have just quit.

I'm interviewing all these fucking assholes. I remember seeing Sal Masekela—the voice of the X Games, ESPN's golden boy—getting to interview LL Cool J, and thinking, *Look—he gets to interview the famous people. Fucking ass-kisser. He fucking can't even skate.* Sal's a cool guy. But I was bitter toward anyone who couldn't skate.

And then some lady was like, "Okay, Jason. Next we have Metallica?" I was like, "What?!" She repeated herself. "Metallica is coming up next, for you to talk to." I struggled to comprehend. But I looked down the line of media, and there they were: James, Kirk, and Lars. It was right after Jason Newsted left the band.

I was shitting a brick. While James and Lars were still talking to other people, Kirk was waiting for them, right next to me. I was like, "Dude, I fucking love you, man. I'm your biggest fan." And he did a head-to-toe on me. *Yeah, sure you are.* Because I was dressed like the FUBU dude in Offspring. And, of course, I'm shitfaced.

I'm trying to convince him that I'm their biggest fan, and then James and Lars come up. I can tell they don't believe me. "Wait, I'll show you," I said. So I'm undoing my belt, and pulling my pants down, and James is looking away, understandably not wanting to see some dude's cock. And then I get the boxer shorts pulled up. Lars licks his finger and runs it over my Metallica tattoo, on my thigh. "It's real!" he says. "Yeah, it's fucking real!" I say. "Group hug!" I formed a huddle with Metallica, James's hand on my back, thinking, *There will be no greater day for me than this day.*

James actually made a joke. He said, "When you pulled your pants down, I figured your tattoo was gonna be somewhere other than your leg. And I figured, if it was where I thought it was, all you would have been able to fit was 'MET.'" And I'm thinking, *Wow, awesome, the God of Metal has just informed me that he thinks I have a small penis!*

I said to James, "Can you give me the 'Go Fast' face?" And right on cue, he raised his eyebrow, just like he does before shit gets hectic onstage at a Metallica show. Amazing that he knew exactly what I was talking about. I mean, he probably doesn't call that face the "Go Fast" face. He probably doesn't even realize he makes a face at all. I felt like our minds had synergized.

Let me remind you, I was *shitfaced.*

I remember my interview with them, though. Unfortunately. "Who do you think's gonna win tonight?" Shit like that. Moron. Fucking pathetic. No questions at all. Although, when you think about it, what *do* you ask a bunch of warlords like Metallica? There's nothing. They're beyond green carpet interviews. I do wish I wasn't dressed like 50 Cent at the time, though. That part I might change.

Later on that night, I saw Hetfield again and I taught him the Rock Lock, which is when you make the devil horns with your hands, and so does someone else, and then you lock devil horns with each other for like a little metal handshake. Colin said he saw them in Vancouver a year later, and James was giving people the Rock Lock. According to Colin, the Rock Lock had therefore caught on through me. (I have video of that, too.) Metallica, you're welcome.

COLIN AND I DID A lot of partying and drinking around then. Generally, his scene was pretty hard to infiltrate. To this day, skateboarders still think it's cool just to be seen standing next to Colin McKay. That's how cool he is.

But we just saw eye to eye. We were very critical of other people's styles. We knew what was up. We could go to clubs and get laid. And a lot of skateboarders couldn't do that. Colin was also one of maybe three vert skaters that were accepted in the street scene. The *real* scene. And because of that, I was accepted. Because I was a Red Dragon, and because I was potentially crazy. Still nowhere near cool enough to be thought of on the level of a street skater myself, mind you. But a lot of the cool guys would at least give me a nod when I was around. Yes, skateboarding is that fucking anal. Because I knew Colin, wore a gold chain, and fucked a bunch of black chicks, I was accepted.

While Sara was still back in Australia, I was all about going to Vegas, to Crazy Girls and a bunch of other strip clubs. I went out with all these black strippers. I would move from one to the other. At that time, almost all my favorite musicians were rappers. I was really into the NBA, too. I wanted to be gangsta. I'm not. I'm a white dude from Sandringham. But when a black chick calls me "her big dick nigga," that's as close as I'm gonna get, and I'll take it.

One of them was in a 50 Cent video. She lived in Inglewood. She had this weird thing where she didn't carry money. If I even asked for some change for a parking meter, she'd say no. Every time she left the house, she went out with zero dollars and zero cents. It's a helluva expectation that someone else is paying for *everything*.

She used to want me to choke her during sex. I was scared to do it. It got to where she would be on top, and I would just hold my arm up, with like a kung fu grip extended, and she would choke herself out on my hand. This chick was not fucking around. One time she burst blood vessels in her face.

That one didn't last long. I actually had a bit of a relationship with a different stripper. She used to purr like a kitten. All the time. In public. At restaurants and stuff. God, she was crazy. I remember we were at some surfer breakfast place one time and Colin McKay showed up with Sal Masekela. This chick was so G'd out it was ridiculous. Gigantic red Gucci sunglasses. Tight-ass Frankie B pants. She had like ten grand worth of bullshit hanging off her. Later on, Sal was like, "Do you realize that you have way more black girlfriends than I've had in my entire life?" Then again, Sal is pretty white for a black dude.

This chick used to tell me she was pregnant whenever she wanted money. Every time we'd break up, she'd be like, "Nigga, I'm pregnant." OK—maybe one time she really was, but not *all* those times.

EVEN THOUGH THE MONEY WAS awesome, it was challenging for me to work for ESPN. It was very hard for me to be an announcer at a contest when I thought I could be in the finals if I just sobered up. Despite being fucked up all the time, I was still extremely good at skateboarding. I still had the ability to beat everybody, every time. At least in my mind. But it got harder for me to get off my ass and go to the ramp every day. For a lot of reasons. Maybe I was sore from skating yesterday. Or maybe I'd been drinking or doing drugs. Or both. Maybe I hadn't slept. And on top of all that, when you get that good at skateboarding, it becomes really hard to learn new tricks. Because everything you know was already so hard to begin with. And now, that incredibly difficult shit you learned last time is just the starting point you have to build off of for the *next* trick.

Skating was a job more than anything at that point. All the way back when I was stuck in Australia, when I started to skate like a street skater, that's when my passion for it started to die. I started simulating street skating on a vert ramp to stay relevant. Out of necessity. But I didn't start skateboarding for that. I wanted to go big, and I wanted to go fast. I have no fucking interest in spending five hours flipping my board until it lands on the right thing on a curb, and then riding away and pretending that I'm a street skater. And the saddest thing is, me learning to do street stuff also permanently screwed up a lot of my vert technique. So I was doubly fucked.

I did set a world record around this time, though. A thirty-six-foot drop-in, near L.A. Danny Way didn't want to do it because they weren't going to pay him enough money. He called me and said, "You wanna make ten grand?" Then I found out it was for the *Guinness Book of World Records*. So there I was. I thought that was the sickest thing ever. I was already a little bit washed up, at least in my mind. I was still considered one of the more stylish skaters, and I still filmed legitimate skate parts. I even got on the cover of *Transworld* around then. But I hadn't been in a contest in two years. So I thought Powell would be happy I was keeping my face out there. "See guys, I'm always working!" Doing this used car salesman dance for my paycheck. It was on TV a bunch. A ton of people called me when it came out.

Not too long after that, I got asked to join DC. Being on DC—that means I'm already slowly admitting that skateboarding is over. I'm stepping out. I'm not actually *skating* for DC—they have Danny Way and Colin McKay, the best skaters in the world. I was just on DC as a court jester. Because I got the approval from Danny and Colin. I was their best friend. They were like, "Fuck yeah, you should pay Ellis." Then I found myself on the reigning team, with the reigning budget. The only bad thing about it was that it made me see how fucked I'd been when I was in my prime. I didn't have a manager, or an agent. I could've made a *lot* more money.

SARA WAS IN AMERICA BY the time I set the world record in 2001. She was there—I think she was even on TV. We would tell each other

"You're the love of my life" and all that, but things between us really weren't any better. She still kept trying to change me. I would get drunk. And then I would get some coke. Sometimes, I could convince Sara to do some. Maybe she would do one line. She wasn't really all that into it, but I could convince her to do that. I was drinking as much as I could, but secretly. I could put up a great front of having it together around Sara, because she wouldn't take any shit. But I was itching to get wasted all the time. Even more so because I wasn't supposed to.

She hated it even if I just smoked weed, because her mum used to smoke bongs in front of her as a kid or something. She had this beef with her mum, which she ended up transferring on to me. Because I think I was similar to her mum. That was the love/hate relationship Sara had with me. She loved me, but I was also the most annoying person on the planet to her at the same time.

Shit just escalated. The more I cleaned up my life, the worse it was if I did go back to my old ways and get drunk with the boys. There would be hell to pay. I don't totally blame her. It must have been torture being married to me. But I was always being controlled, and yelled at, like I was a stupid little boy. It was ridiculous. I mean, she wouldn't even let me jack off. I used to hide it from her, because I knew she didn't like it.

We were staying in this weird little studio apartment in Carlsbad, near the water. It was a real rickety little room with pretty much just a bed in it. But Sara didn't mind. We used to go down near the water and play with crabs all day. One time, outside this place, we were arguing again over drinking and smoking weed. I told her I wasn't gonna quit. "I can't," I think I said. At that point, I had already accepted that I was eventually going to fade out. And my wife—all one hundred twenty pounds of her—punched me in the face. I didn't see it coming at all. I was in shock. When I realized what had happened, I was instantly like, "You're fucking joking me. I want a fucking divorce, you idiot."

"You have no idea who you're fucking with," she said. In an instant, her voice had changed into this weird, evil, I'm-tougher-than-you thing. She was threatening me. She was almost grunting the words. "I'll do whatever I want, and you will not dare to cross me, or I will make your fucking life a living hell." Holy massive mistake. I couldn't believe what I'd gotten myself into. I was terrified.

I told her okay. My brain couldn't get past it. *Well,* I thought, *if I'm fucked, and my life is going to be hell if I leave you, then I . . . guess I better stay, right?*

People always talk about girls changing after you marry them, but that one was a real shocker. The one eighty that Sara pulled was unbelievable. It was like I'd signed a contract, and now she was going to use it against me.

You might be thinking there was some part of me that thought I deserved to get hit, or secretly liked it or something. But trust me—I never got off on getting beat up. Having someone be mad at me is my least favorite thing in the world. I may find a lot of ways to get physically injured in my life, but believe it or not, it's not something I go around looking for. I know I should have left Sara the first time she hit me, but I stayed for the same reason I always stayed with girls: I was terrified of being alone. I needed someone to take care of me.

So I stuck around. And the beatings continued. It calmed down after that first time. She apologized the next day. She had a crazy temper. But then those instances would happen again. Maybe four or five times a year. It escalated more and more. I mean, this wasn't little stuff. She would punch me in the face, a lot. When I would come home wasted, which was a lot of the time, she would hit me, mercilessly. Of course I would never hit her back. And she knew it.

I told my friends, and they all thought I was joking. Another time, Sara and me were staying with my friend, Matthias, a pro skateboarder. He had a really nice house, so we moved out of that little studio in Carlsbad and into a bedroom in his place. One day I came back from hanging out at someone else's house. I'd been smoking weed and playing video games. That's what I did in the afternoon when I wasn't skating. This was the lifestyle that I had lived for so long.

So I come back, and she's like, "Are you high?" I told her no. I've got sunglasses on, inside the house. "I just feel like wearing them," I told her. "Take your fucking sunglasses off," she said. She would automatically just talk to me like that. Like my father. That whole cussing, aggressive thing. So I gave in and took my glasses off.

I was on my stomach a few minutes later to play a video game. She walked right over to me, leaned down, and punched me in the face. Then she was jumping up and down on my back and on my head. Like she was trying to foot stomp my head into the ground. While she was going for one of her foot stomps, I caught something moving up the staircase out of the corner of my eye. I looked, and it was Matthias, running up the stairs to his bedroom, fleeing the scene of my wife attacking me in his living room.

From that day on, he was like, "You've gotta be fucking kidding me, dude. You can't take that." He hadn't believed me when I told him what was going on. "Why would you not believe me?" I said. "Why would I make up that some little white chick is beating me up?" She was probably like five six with C-cup boobies. She was a model, you know? A stripper.

After that one, at Matthias's house, I told her, "I'm really gonna divorce you." But then she said she would go to anger management. I figured that if she was admitting there was a problem, then maybe we could work something out.

We weren't around each other all the time, because of my job. Being on the road made it easy for me to cheat on Sara, especially when I started to get recognized from being on TV. One time, during the X Games, I actually needed two hotel rooms to pull off my advanced sexual maneuvers. I met a girl who worked at the hotel restaurant and invited her up to my room. While I waited for her to get off work and come upstairs, I went to a club at the hotel, met two chicks there, got a *second* room, ordered champagne for all of us, and fucked both of them. After that I met the girl from the restaurant in the first room and fucked her there. But then I was like, "I've got to go handle some business," or something brilliant like that, and went back downstairs. I bought a bunch of drinks at the bar to take back up, because I could never wait for room service. (I would order drinks to drink while I waited for my drinks. Makes sense, right?) But while I was at the bar, I saw this absolute clown-ass DJ that I used to fuck. Tattoos on her pussy, Aryan blond head, kinda thick—more or less a female me. I was tweaked, and I wanted to fuck her again. So I did.

What is it that they call it when you basically want to fuck yourself? Narcissistic?

TV DICKHEAD

The announcing job was actually start-ing to take off. No one cared that I was drinking all the time. If anything, it helped. Nobody knew how far it went. And a couple times I went out partying with big, high-up ESPN dudes. Smoking weed and drinking all night in Town Cars. Hooking up with chicks. In the end, I might have kept my job an extra year or two because somebody's boss's boss thought I was cool.

The same dude that hired me for ESPN suggested me for Tony Hawk's Gigantic Skatepark Tour. This was a tremendous honor. From the lowest of lows for skateboarding to the highest of highs, Tony Hawk has always been on the same pedestal to me. Massive. Almost godlike. And the way ESPN had planned it, the Gigantic Skatepark Tour would be the closest any vert skater had gotten to being a legitimate rock star. If you're a pro skater, and you were on that tour, that's the greatest thing you've ever been a part of. It was a rock-and-roll tour. I've seen 50 Cent's tour bus, and it was exactly the same as ours was. Flatscreens inside the bus and everything. Only we had two of them.

I had my corner on the party bus, with my video games and my weed. We never got shut down. For anything. If Andy McDonald or one of the more mellow skaters wanted us to shut up, he got sent to the front of the bus and told to deal with it. I've never been able to figure out why I wasn't kicked off, much less invited back to every single tour. For three years.

ESPN had a budget and they had ideas. It was like, "Today we're gonna jump out of planes" or "Today we're gonna race NASCARs." It was a skateboard tour that occasionally stopped to wrestle crocodiles. And it was all on TV. It wasn't just a job—we all got a whole new career out of it. The money took off, again. I used to get three hundred a month off Dragon sunglasses, and then all of a sudden I got fifteen hundred a month, because I was on TV all year. All told, I was making like twelve grand a month. Way more money than I was capable of handling at this point of my life. On my thirtieth birthday, in a hotel in Vegas, I made a line of coke into the shape of Australia. I did the whole thing by myself. (It was pretty much a solo night. Any companions that may have been there were being *paid* to hang out with me.) I also drank a bottle of Cristal that Tony Hawk gave me. He wasn't anywhere near my shenanigans, obviously—he sent it through a friend.

Tony just liked us crazy guys, so we had right of way. He obviously has a lot of responsibilities, being Tony Hawk. It's possible he just liked knowing that someone else was bringing a little danger and edginess to the shows. Or maybe he just kept me around because he thought I was funny. Sometimes, at bars, I would get him laughing until he literally fell over on the ground. And then I would still be hitting him with some stupid jokes, to keep him down there. Maybe it was that simple.

We traveled the world. I stayed in my own hotel room in Paris for like a week, including possibly the greatest night in my life. It began at a club, where someone gave me ecstasy. As we were heading somewhere else, on our way out there was this little dude with a posse trying to fight with security. We got a little bit farther away, and suddenly I heard *POP! POP! POP! POP!* Everyone hit the ground. One of the dude's dudes had run to his Ferrari to grab a gun and then opened fire on the bouncers.

We ran for our lives, and then we caught a taxi and went to this other club that was on a boat. There was a back room. The roof was really low, and everyone was hunched over, smoking hash joints. I smoked enough that I convinced myself I could understand the French language. There were these strippers there. One of them had metal teeth and red stars tattooed on her nipples. As in, her nipples themselves were actually tattooed. Needless to say I fell in love with her instantly. She was branded, in this crazy wide pattern, all the way around one of her thighs.

She had a friend, and there was this guy there that told the friend to show me her vagina. At least, that's what I heard him say, now that I officially spoke French. She pulled down her panties and showed me her cookie, which had a forest tattooed on it.

The girls were being really nice to me, and kissing me, and then they took me to this little VIP area by a stage. I was in there by myself as they went out and did this weird fire sex show. They had these fireball things sticking off their shoulders, and they would spit on the fire and send flames flying wherever they wanted. They spit fire over my head, and I felt the lamp oil fall all over me like a warm blanket.

I couldn't convince the metal teeth girl to have sex with me, so I went back to the hotel. At that point, this already qualified as one of the greatest nights of my life. But then, as I was paying for the taxi, I passed this amazing black chick that was on her way out. She had been hitting on me earlier at the bar. She got in a car, but I yelled back at her, so she got out and came back inside with me.

We had a few drinks then went back to my room, where she informed me that she was a prostitute. Of course, to a guy like me that was not a problem. The sun was coming up and shining through the window as she straddled me. She was standing up, doing this swivel thing with her hips and vagina. Quite possibly the most impressive sex maneuver I had seen in my life.

I gave her all my money. Who knows how much. It was euro dollars. Francs, I guess. It was like Monopoly money to me. Here, there's an orange one, and a blue one, too. Have all of them. I don't care.

Man, I really like Tony Hawk.

I was really paid by ESPN to be the announcer on the tour, but I refused to be that guy. Sure, I did the TV interviews. And I probably made them more entertaining than your average skateboarder could have. That was my job. They kept me on there for that. But I padded up with all the other skaters. I never just grabbed a microphone. I skated every single demo.

My whole stunt guy, jumping-off-things reputation really took hold on those tours. Because Tony was so amazingly good. Put it this way—my grand finale ride was his *first* ride. I couldn't really stop drinking at this point. And it was to the point now where I couldn't skate as well as I used to because of it. Starting around the time I was doing heroin, for the first time in my life, I felt insecure on the ramp. I could still hold my own, but I was really just coasting on the skills I had built up years ago. I wasn't getting better. I wasn't even staying at the same level. I was getting worse.

So I thought of other ways to stay relevant on the ramp. What do I have to offer? What's gonna keep me paid? It really was a less enjoyable time as a skater because I was just doing it for money. I was creative enough and dangerous enough to jump off stuff. So I would just find a rafter, and then fly off the fucking thing.

Sometimes these jumps were not that difficult or dangerous. And sometimes I would get up to wherever I was gonna jump from, and I would have to give myself a talking-to: *You have gotten yourself in some fucking shit now, dude. Go to your happy place. If you do this, but you hesitate, you're going to break your leg. So you may as well completely commit.* I would have to argue with common sense, until common sense would go away. Only then could I commit one hundred percent to jumping into something where I thought my leg might snap.

Once I figured that out, I would use that line of thinking on a whole bunch of stuff. I use it a lot now. If there's a place I need to go where things seem like they might get really bad—like having a humongous snake bite me on the radio—I can just convince the smart person inside of me to go away until it's over, to get the job done.

The older I got, the more that had to happen. And the older I got, the crazier I got. I don't think people realized that. Back in the day, people thought I was crazy, but I was just stupid. I didn't know you could get brain damage from getting knocked out a lot. So who gives a shit? Every day, for twenty years, I woke up knowing, for a fact, that I was going to slam that day. But now the stunts were getting bigger. The slams were getting worse. I'd woken up from surgeries in agony.

Pain so bad I would do anything to not be living inside my body at that moment. I'd been knocked out so hard that I couldn't see for a while. Knocked out to the point where it made me emotional. Crying in the shower and shit like that.

If skateboarding's gonna be like that, it's only a matter of time before you realize maybe skateboarding isn't worth it. Meanwhile, the ESPN gig was growing. Amazingly enough, they tried giving me a TV show, too. One episode, anyway. My agent hooked it up. *The Jason Ellis Show: My Job Sucks.* I don't remember a bunch of meetings or anything like that. It was just, "We're gonna do a TV show. We're gonna give you a pilot and run it on ESPN2." And I was like, "Cool."

I remember smoking a bunch of weed and showing up to the DC ramp. They made a desk out of coping, and they were like, "OK—go." They had a basketball hoop and my guitar, and I had my bandannas and my sunglasses, and I interviewed Danny Way.

Pink was on it, too. This was just after Pink met Carey Hart. That's how it came together. The whole Carey–Steve Astephen angle. I knew Carey from Big Day Out or Warped Tour in Australia. He was over there riding moto, and I was there skating. This was when I had just met Sara. I grew up riding moto, so I befriended him. He let me have a go on his bike in the parking lot, and we've been friends ever since.

I was on top of the vert ramp at X Games the first time Pink showed up there. I was announcing. *Fuck, I blew it,* I thought. *I should be in there competing so that Pink could see me and I might be able to date her.* That night I heard that Carey was going out with her. That's fair enough. He's better looking.

For my TV show, I showed up at her house with a camera crew, and I was like, "Hey—you're Pink!" And then she dyed my hair pink. As you can see, this was high-caliber television. I didn't know what the fuck I was doing.

I'm offensive to myself when I look at it now, seeing what an opportunity I had then, and how I dealt with it. Now, if I got a TV show, I would probably be dieting and cleansing for a month beforehand. Back then, I literally ashed one out as I walked in front of the camera.

The pilot had three guests. It was Danny Way, and Pink, and then I went to San Francisco to interview Jason Richardson, a basketball player who'd just won the slam dunk contest. I was out all night the night before I met him. The film crew abandoned me. I ended up finding an African club. Not African American. Like, hard-core Zimbabwe style. They had chicken wings and shit like that, and I ended up getting shit hammered by myself. The only white boy in there. Dressed like a black dude. But like a tool. Like Offspring. Hitting on chicks. Like fifty-five-year-old fat black women, until I eventually pulled somebody who couldn't believe how stupid a white boy would be. I woke up in a room somewhere. No idea what happened.

The next morning, the film guy was like, "You look like shit." They put Preparation H under my eyes to take down the swelling. I was stinking up a storm at this basketball hoop, playing one-on-one with Jason Richardson. No idea. No script. No anything. I didn't say one funny thing or do anything that would give you any inkling that I had any talent whatsoever. I did score one point against Jason Richardson one-on-one, for what that's worth.

When I got back home, some of my friends came over and we watched the show on TV. I bought a bottle of Cristal and we smoked weed all night and that was the end of it. I was back to my announcing gigs.

Obviously, ESPN paid me a lot of money for a job that was not all that difficult. But at that point, to me, the TV people were a big problem. The reason they pulled me off my vert ramp in Australia is because I could talk. I was creative. I could say a lot of hilarious shit.

But then, the more I started to flex that at skate events, the more they started to shut it down. And the more I started to get pissed, the more I would say things I shouldn't be saying. You know, drunk, or hungover. "Fuck that guy! He's a fucking idiot!" With a mike in my hand. No idea that the mike was on. No idea that the fucking idiot I was talking about could hear everything. So I ended up pissing some people off. I was desperate to get out of that job. Eventually, I hated it, even though I did it for like five years.

I was very jealous seeing friends of mine compete, while I had a microphone, and a boss, and had to go to meetings. I wasn't a TV guy. I was a skateboarder. I really saw the ugly side of ESPN, and how skateboarders were nothing but a cash cow. I don't know about now, but at least at that time, the main people in X Games straight up hated skateboarding. They really wanted to work for baseball but had been given this shit job instead. I heard them say it. "Jose Canseco is a way better athlete than Bob Burnquist." I remember having an argument with one of my bosses about it.

Or they would say, "If you talk about Shaun White more, we get higher ratings." If you've ever watched the Summer *or* Winter X Games, you obviously know that ESPN can *not* get enough of the Flying Tomato. I made up that nickname, by the way. This was years ago. I was announcing Shaun at a demo or a contest or something, and I remember his mum was there. He was maybe fourteen. And I was making fun of him, because his mummy was standing there. Not in a mean way. She was laughing, too. I was like, "It must be pretty cool to have your mummy here. If you get hurt, she can put some ice on your knee, or maybe get you a sandwich." There were maybe twenty people there, and they were all giggling. Out of nowhere, I was just like, "Look at him, Mummy—he's like a little flying tomato." Then Sal Masekela jumped on that one like a fucking hotcake and took it to the bank. I have no problem with that. Sal and I used to be roommates on the Tony Hawk tours, and over the years, I put Sal through a lot of hell that he did not deserve at all.

I was a mess of a person at this point. And then to make matters worse, my dog, Grimey, disappeared. I was out on tour, in Texas I think. Sara called me, freaking out. "He's gone! He's gone!" He got loose and got eaten by a coyote. I had never faced death before. I never had lost anyone I loved that much, except maybe my grandma. I really loved Grimey. It sent me into a tailspin. I was at a bar. Hysterical. Bawling. People couldn't calm me down. Out on the street, on the ground, crying.

And once again, that DJ chick with tattoos on her vagina was around. She was always around for me whenever I wanted her, out on the road. I was at the bar, drinking double vodka cranberries. Fucking chugging them. And she was on the other side of the bar, trying to help me. "Are you okay?" I was like, "My dog! Just make the pain go away!" So off we went to the hotel room, to make the pain go away for twenty minutes. I remember passing out, and then waking up in the morning. It was a big one for me, losing Grimey. I got a tattoo of his name on the inside of my right wrist, right where I used to carry him. I had him on my helmet for the longest time.

Continuing on after the Gigantic Skatepark Tour, whenever I'd get on tour, I'd still cheat on Sara if I could. I didn't necessarily go looking for it, but I definitely didn't turn down many opportunities. I had sex with a Russian Olympic gold medalist chick. Someone I met at X Games. They had her there to hang out with X Games medalists in the athlete lounge. For a while, we had this whole weird relationship thing going, where I would call and some Russian dude would answer the phone, "YOU NOT CALL HERE ANYMORE." I assumed it was a boyfriend. She swore it was her coach. Then she left a message on my phone. Sara caught it and, as you might imagine, kicked the shit out of me again.

My marriage obviously wasn't going too well. Neither was skating. Announcing was keeping me paid, but killing me on the inside. My ultimate goal became being alone. Getting all the cocaine, all the booze, all the weed, all the red wine, everything I wanted, into the DC ramp. I had a tent there, and there was a band room, too. It was in Vista, out in the middle of nowhere, so the cops were never going to come. I didn't want anyone with me. I would just play drums and guitar, and do lines and smoke bongs and cigarettes. All night. All day. I would lock myself in there at least once a week. And after one of those marathons, it was always very hard to make myself want to recover and go skate.

One time me and Sara had a fight. Since I had a key to the ramp, I locked myself in there so she couldn't get to me. I just lived there for a while. Colin and Danny were cool with that, because they knew my wife was a fucking psychopath. Once I would finally pass out, and then come to, my mouth would be burning, because I hadn't had any water for so long. The first sip, my mouth would hurt. I got used to that. Bracing myself for it. "Here we go." Because I was so fucked.

In the midst of all this, I took part in the motion picture extravaganza *Zolar,* about an extreme skateboarding alien. My agent hooked it up. They were filming in Vancouver, so all it meant to me was a free flight up there. Vancouver was like Vegas to me. The only thing that's remarkable about the movie shoot is how many drugs I took the day before they shot my part. I took every drug there is. GHB. Cocaine. Weed. Drinking. I did not sleep at all for two days straight. *Zolar* is a children's movie. I do *not* recommend it.

The last straw with Sara happened when DC flew us out to Aspen. We were staying in this massive apartment with tons of rooms, so there were other people staying there as well. I had to go to an autograph signing at a bar and then hang out after. Free drinks and all that. Obviously I was looking at it as an opportunity to get shit-faced, but technically, it was also my job, and she knew that. "Make sure you're back by twelve," she said.

I didn't come back until closing time. By myself. Wasted. She was right on me at the door to our room, calling me a stupid cunt. "Fuck off," I said, not even thinking. I wasn't even looking at her when I said it. And then—*WHAM*—a kick in the nuts. Never saw it coming. That bent me over. And then, a full-on boot to the face. Thus far in our relationship, this was easily the best shot she'd ever given me. To the point where, to tell the truth, I was a little bit rocked. I didn't know it then, but I know it now that I've been fighting for a while: I was on queer street.

When I came out of the haze from that, she was already rabbit-punching me. Repeated blows, raining down on my neck. But by then, I had gotten sick of flinching. She would always cock her hand and flinch me. She was all of maybe a buck twenty, and here I've been, flinching, like a bitch. So I just let her little beatdown happen.

There was blood pouring out of my face everywhere. I went into the living room to lie down. She followed me in. "What the fuck are you doing?" I guess I didn't have a very good answer. She stayed right on me. "Get the fuck in the bedroom, right now!" So I did. I went to bed and went to sleep and when I woke up, my pillow was covered in blood. My face had been bleeding all night.

What I didn't know was that another guy had heard the whole incident. A professional photographer who'd been hired by DC to come along. To this day, when I run into the guy, I know this is what he thinks of as soon as he sees me—me being beaten within an inch of my life by my stripper wife.

When he saw me the next morning, he couldn't believe I was alive. Obviously my face was messed up. "Dude, you can't take that shit," he said. "I thought she was murdering you." I still might have let it go, but the photographer told another guy at DC, and then that guy confronted me, too. I pleaded her case for her. "She's gonna go to anger management!" I said. "No, dude," he said. "Anybody that does that, it's over."

I again told her I wanted a divorce. This time it finally stuck. I didn't even get a lawyer. I just gave her half my money for a year and a half, because we'd been married for three years. That was the deal we worked out. At the time, it was a lot of money.

We had bought a house in Vista. She picked it out. I had told her to get whatever one she liked. I didn't even see it until it was already ours. I gave her the house and stayed at other people's places until she moved out and went back to Australia.

COCAINE IS REALLY
BAD FOR YOU

Sara's first move after we got divorced was to immediately start fucking a guy that worked with my agent. What I didn't know was that, while we were married, my friend had propositioned her, and that she fucked him in Matthias's house. Right in that same living room where she beat me up, actually. It was a really good friend of mine. I didn't find this out until we got divorced. Not that I had been remotely faithful, obviously.

One time, not long after Sara and I broke up, I had some chick over, and in the middle of the night I heard some noises around the back of the house where I was staying. I had a gun at the time. I thought I needed a Glock, for some reason. Listening to too much hip-hop I guess. I had gotten it off some sketchy dude. I had never owned a gun before. I used them as a kid, but they were all my dad's. I had never even shot this thing.

But when I heard the noises, I grabbed the gun, and I'm following the sound. Up the side of the house, around to the back, and then up the stairs to a glass sliding door. Then there's Sara's head, and she's looking up at me. The gun is in my hand, pointed at her face. Maybe six inches away. "We need to fucking talk!" she said. Gun to her face. She never blinked. "I heard you've been talking shit!" I somehow managed to send her on her way. She went peacefully. For her, anyway.

WHEN I BROKE UP WITH Sara, Rachel flew in from New York to hang out with me. I think she thought we were going to get back together. Just like old times.

I sent a limo to pick her up and bring her to Matthias's house. Her face was all swollen on one side. She was a little bit chunky. We did tons of coke. She tried to grab a poisonous spider out of a tank. I was like, "What are you doing?" Even on a bunch of coke, I was not that gangster. She was all outback about it. "Ah, she'll be all right, mate." And then she tried to fight Matthias. She was strangling him. I realized that I had evolved, at least a little bit. Rachel was a moron. That was the last time I ever considered dating her again.

I moved on to this millionaire chick, for like a minute. Her dad owned a NASCAR team. They had a massive house and a massive boat. The boat had *other* boats on it that it could crane out onto the water. It had its own captain, too. We wanted to take the boat out one time, and she had to call the captain so he could come over from the apartment they gave him. The family was crazy religious. She was constantly trying to fuck me in front of them, and I wouldn't do it. It was a typical case of a good Christian girl rebelling from her upbringing and trying to go out with a bad boy. Even *I* knew it.

Somehow Colin and I ended up in the Vin Diesel masterpiece *Triple X*. My agent arranged that one, too. I had cool tattoos and stuff—that's why they picked me. It was me, Colin, Carey Hart, and Mike Vallely. When we were filming it, me and Colin and our friend Sam stayed in a hotel, up near Sacramento. We were at some bar, drinking. And then we got kicked out. Colin kicked a random car in the parking lot. I ran and shoulder blocked it. And then Sam ran up and focused the back windscreen. Then we all ran off. Somebody threw a chair through a plateglass window at a Taco Bell down the road from the hotel. And then I went to my room, hiding. Meanwhile, Sam and Colin went on a Red Dragon tear, trashing their room to the point where, when Colin woke up in the morning, he went to the bathroom to wash his face, turned the tap on, and the water poured straight down to the carpet, because they'd smashed the sink out.

They had to pay a bunch of money for the damage to the hotel. But Colin had more money than any other vert skater on the planet. When they confronted him, he just said, "Here's a credit card. Put a fucking fruit basket on there for yourself, too." Once again, Red Dragons.

The movie experience was a great big nothing. I was just faded by then. We didn't even care, at all. *Yeah, great, we're on a movie set. Who gives a shit.* Although I do believe, honest to God, that Vin Diesel stole my look from me, on the set of *Triple X*. All I can tell you is that I was dressed a certain way—like a rock-and-roll skateboarder, with a lot of jewelry, and a beret, and a jacket with a fur collar. Meanwhile, Vin Diesel was dressed like a weightlifter who went to the gym too much. And then the next time I saw him, he was dressed exactly like me. And I know he saw me. I have witnesses. I remember the Vin Diesel look that he gave me when I met him at the bar. The best way I can describe it is that, at the time, I thought that maybe he wanted to fuck me. There was this sort of smirk on his face. He was kind of sizing me up and nodding at me for a long time. But I also live in my own lunch box, so that could be completely wrong.

That was the last major event in my life that happened while I still had hair. I was a bandanna guy by the time I was in *Triple X*. Facing the reality of my receding hairline, I shaved my head right afterward. I had seen it coming for a long time, and I was ready. But that was a sad day.

I didn't have a wife. I didn't have a dog. I wasn't really skating. But I was still getting paid by ESPN, at least for a little while longer. They were committed to putting a bunch of skateboarding on TV, and I was the only skateboarder who could actually talk that was accepted by all the other skaters. This was a time when certain skaters would literally walk away from an ESPN reporter, rather than talk to some kook on TV. We were punk rock. We were cooler than everyone, as far as we were concerned. If I was gone, ESPN might not get any more interviews. So they had to keep me. There was nothing to stop me.

AFTER I GOT DIVORCED, COCAINE really started to rule my existence. Thanks to this period of my life, my nostrils are no longer even. I have a really big hole on one side, and a really little hole on the other. Some people might talk about being on cocaine like it's some kind of nonstop living nightmare. But it wasn't, for me. At the time, I definitely thought my life was extremely awesome. I could party all the time. I could get anything I wanted. I thought it was ridiculously awesome to be able to get a bunch of coke and then do all of it. Although all I really have to show for it is a bunch of fucktarded stories.

I remember being at a skateboarding trade show in San Diego. I spent three days across the street in a hotel room doing bumps. I never slept and never once went to the show. There was this other guy there that kept saying, "I gotta get out of here!" For three straight days he said that. He never left the hotel room either. By the third day, I was finally nodding off, but every time I started to fall asleep, he would wake me up by blasting more coke. Then he would apologize. And then tell me he had to get out of there. He'd been sweating so much, he looked like a glazed donut. I was a pro skater, across the street from a trade show. I could have been plowing every female down there. But instead I was hanging out with a fucking glazed donut and a bag of coke. I would just do a bunch of coke, then smoke a bunch of weed and drink a bunch of red wine to bring myself back down. Over and over. For three straight days.

And then there was the time I went out to the desert. Who knows where. There was a massive party out there with Danny Way and his whole crew. I'd never been to the desert before. And I've never been back. This was the only time. I drove out there from San Diego in my 740iL. I had a bag of cocaine under my seat in a do-rag, because I heard about doing that in a Noreaga song.

So at the campfire, I drank a bunch of vodka and then Danny invited me to ride his Banshee. Those guys didn't know me as a moto dude, so I was thinking I would surprise everyone with my skills. We went up some hill and Danny bailed on a jump. To show him what a massive pussy he was, I went for it. I just remember being in the air for a *really* long time before I bailed, over the handlebars. I crashed it pretty good. I think I wound up owing Danny money over that.

We were drinking, and I lost track of everyone I knew there, and then people started to leave. It was getting late. I tried to hitch a ride, and no one wanted to pick me up because I was so plastered. I was begging the last group of people. "Please don't leave me here!" But they left me out in the middle of nowhere. To die.

It was really cold. I was pretty sure I was about to go into shock. There was no road anywhere. I was just wandering around in sand, by moonlight, until I saw some car headlights.

I started running toward the lights. I was screaming to get their attention. It was a Jeep. "You've gotta help me!" I said. They agreed to give me a lift. They were willing to take me to the campsite, but I had no idea where that was. I'd only been there for like ten minutes, before we all went to party in this other spot. "Just take me to the road," I said.

I found my car, and I told the guy to leave me there. But I had left the keys at the campsite. It was freezing. I was running laps around my car, just trying to stay warm. And I was so tired. I found a tractor tire, and I slept inside that for a while, trying to stay alive until the sun came up. Somebody found me and got me my car keys.

Everyone was laughing at me the next day. Colin asked me, "Why didn't you just focus the window and sleep in your car?" "Because it was a BMW!" I said. "I'm supposed to kick in the window, you rich spoiled prick?" Colin is so rich, it turns out even his survival tactics are elitist.

And then there was the time I ate a shark's heart.

If I could take this whole thing back, I totally would. It wasn't my idea. I'd been awake for two days. We were in Mexico, fishing. Danny Way loved to fish. I've never been a fisherman in my entire life. I was just there because I had been told that other guys were bringing more drugs than anyone could possibly run out of. So I was in.

All I wanted to do was catch a shark. Because I love sharks. At that point, I was not yet able to use my brain to put two and two together and realize that loving sharks and killing sharks was a little bit hypocritical.

My obsession with sharks was known well enough that as soon as they had one on the line, my name came up immediately. All of a sudden, someone yelled, "Ellis, we've got a shark!" They gave me that big rod that sits in a harness on your stomach. You pull it, and then reel, and then pull it, and then reel. Over and over. There was at least a solid hour of reeling this thing in. A five-foot thrasher shark. It was an amazing battle. Danny Way and all those dudes were nice enough to let me have the opportunity.

Before I move on to the next part of the story, let me remind you again how casually shitfaced everybody was. At one point, there was a humongous grouper fish chilling by the side of the boat, and while everyone was standing there admiring it, a massive fat naked dude jumped off the roof of the boat and body-slammed the fish. While he was in the water, the fish bit him or something, and then he scrambled back into the boat, naked, with his shriveled up little cocaine dick.

Anyway, I finally pulled the shark out. It was a big-ass beast. Everyone went nuts. There was a crew on the boat. One of them was a former skater who had become a fisherman. That's why we were there in the first place. For some legal reason, they had to sever the nerves in the shark's head before they brought it on the boat. And then they cut out the heart, and someone was holding it. It was still beating. So I grabbed it out of his hand and bit it in half. I could feel the heart beating as it went down my throat. I started screaming, "I've got the heart of a shark!" with blood all over my hands. Someone wrote the Red Dragons logo on my shirt in blood. They put it in a Red Dragons video. See if you can spot me—I'm the guy with the shark's head on top of my own head. I was kind of known for that for a while.

I don't like that the clip is still on YouTube, glorifying that moment. But it happened. And I'll spend the rest of my radio life telling people that they should *not* drink so much that they end up eating a shark's heart. I don't want to kill sharks. I don't even want to kill a cow. I will if I'm starving, for protein purposes, but I love animals.

By the tail end of my cocaine life, I remember going to parties, and then just standing there sweating. I didn't even want anybody to talk to me. I just wanted to get in a room, hit the coke, then the weed and red wine to take the edge off, and repeat. That was all I wanted. I was ridiculous. If there was a girl who wanted to come with me and play with my shrunken flaccid cocaine penis, awesome. Bonus. If not, you fuck off, too. It was like a slow suicide.

When you're down in the shit like that, it's amazing the people that find you. I did have some sweet-ass friends at the end there. There was this coke dealer. He didn't have one of his hands. There was a time where I had done so much coke it had eaten the inside of my nose, and I couldn't do any more. It was bleeding so much it prevented me from any further snorting. I was breathing through my mouth, and my tongue was hanging out. He suggested I smoke it instead. This seemed fishy. "Isn't that crack?" I asked. But he told me that was freebasing. This was great news. It's not crack? Well then, what's the problem?

I disappeared into my room. I was staying in a room at my friend's house. Yet another skater friend's house, after Matthias. I'm not sure he knew what I was doing in there. I lit candles, and let them burn down into the carpet. I had these pet mice that had been breeding and breeding, untold generations, until they were almost pouring out of the tank they were in. They were eating each other. I was watching them do it. I had this cassette player, and I would listen to Metallica and Faith No More, over and over again. The major thought on my mind was, *Man, it's so awesome that now I can keep doing coke even after my nose is blown out.*

That was the first time I ever had heart palpitations. Later on that became a recurring problem. But at the time, I just made a joke about it and put it behind me. I thought I was indestructible.

I also had ball pythons, when I was staying at yet another skater's house, still during my cocaine era. They had names for sure, but fucked if I remember. I went on a tour, and when I came back, they had escaped, so I figured they were dead. But one time I was on a lot of coke, and I was looking in the mirror, popping zits and pulling nose hairs out, and next thing I know—there's a snake! It was in a cupboard behind me, and it was peering out. I'm in mid zit-pop and suddenly a snake is dangling over my shoulder. I saw it in the reflection. I hit the deck. It took me a second to recover and realize that this was *my* snake. And then I went to go to bed, and I stepped on the other one, under the blankets. Having snakes was a bad idea for me.

Cocaine just takes over. At first, my friends and I would get some coke, and then we would go out. And then, we would go out less. And then, we would just sit around a table and do cocaine. That *was* our whole night. I remember I hung out with this masseuse chick one time. She had some beach house for the night, and I fucked her. She wanted to get some coke, so I went and grabbed a gram from the do-rag in my car. Straight off the bat, I blasted like half of it off the table. She was appalled. "Holy shit," she said. "That's the biggest bump I've ever seen in my life!" I'm not sure what the technical definition of a "bump" is, but this one was as wide as my thumb. "You've got a problem," she said. I was like, "How can you already tell I've got a problem? We just got the drugs." To her way of thinking, snorting half a gram in half a second was enough proof that I was beyond a recreational drug user. I was genuinely surprised. That thought had honestly not occurred to me until then.

I tried to quit several times. After she said that, I only really did coke when I got so drunk that it wasn't really me making the decisions anymore. "Whoo! You know a guy that can get drugs?! Whoo!" And then as soon as it went up my nose, I'd have a moment of clarity. *Oh. Right. I wasn't gonna do this anymore, was I?* I think that happened maybe three more times.

You could say that was rock bottom. Although truthfully, there were tons of rock bottoms. Throughout my pro career, oftentimes I was forced to clean up, just to make sure I would place at a contest, just to make sure my sponsors wouldn't drop me. The trouble was, whenever I managed to pull that off, I would then stage an epic, never-ending celebration because of it, and start the vicious cycle all over again.

Once or twice, at the strong suggestion of the legal authorities, I had even tried AA, but they lost me as soon as they got to the God stuff. At that point in my life, I was pretty sure God wasn't real. (Although I've started to come around.) So if I needed him to do AA, well, then AA is out.

It was skateboarding that saved my life. Yet again. I knew I was washed up. I knew it was over. But I still needed to skate, on some level. And the amount of drugs I was taking was keeping me from getting to the ramp. At all. Ever. I literally never saw daylight. But because of that need to skate that was still inside of me, from time to time I would make myself stop and sober up, and get the shit out of my system for a week so that I could skate.

I remember predicting the end of skateboarding for myself long before it was actually true. I remember telling Danny Way, "I've probably got two more years." And he would just laugh his face off. "We're forever in this game." For some reason, he held me on the same level as him. Maybe Danny Way was forever, but I sure as hell wasn't. And in my defense, I was pretty much right.

But the MegaRamp did get me one last little golden era. The MegaRamp was Danny pushing it to the limits. Going bigger. Changing the game. That was Danny's thing, building off what Matt Hoffman did in BMX. Before Danny made the MegaRamp, Matt made a massive quarter pipe, got towed in by a dirt bike, and did a fucking twenty-foot air. That was in 1993, before anybody had done anything like that.

Danny Way is the greatest skateboarder that ever lived, in my opinion. At this point, he was over being in contests. Which worked out great for me, because so was I. The last few contests I was in, the same story kept repeating itself. Me almost making Kickflip 540s. The announcer going "OHHH! He *almost* made it!" And me getting knocked out. With my lifestyle and my age, I couldn't keep going to the concussion party. But I needed those massive 540s to compete. My thing was going big and keeping it real. I was too old to jump on the next trendy bandwagon of tricks.

So the MegaRamp had my name written all over it. I was on that thing with bells on. I was the second person ever to jump it. I wasn't thinking about competing. It wasn't in the X Games yet. I was just excited. You went so much faster, and so much bigger than on a vert ramp. That meant more hang time, which meant better tricks. Just the thought that the greatest skateboard trick I would ever do had yet to come was inspirational. I thought for sure that had already happened. But you could go so big on the MegaRamp—who knows what I could do on that thing?

I filmed a video part for Red Dragons on the MegaRamp. I had all these ledge tricks. There was a camera guy who just stayed there and would shoot me for like an hour straight, waiting to capture the perfect ride. That was the first time in my career I ever had that. It had been five years since I'd been relevant as a skater, but I remember a lot of people saying that that was a legitimate video part.

This was in 2004, right around when my radio career began. The only reason I'm on the air today is because Tony Hawk wanted me on his Sirius show, *Demolition Radio*. I may have been off cocaine, but at this point in my life, very few people were thinking, "Let's give that man a radio show!" But for some insane reason, Tony Hawk was.

Yet another low point of me getting wasted coincided with one of the early episodes of Tony's show, all of which was also filmed for Carey Hart's TV show, *Inked*.

We were in Las Vegas. I had been drinking all day. Our guest was Chuck Liddell. I decided to do everything I could to get Chuck to punch me. And not a little love tap. When he finally did punch me, I knew he pulled it, so I made him do it again. For real. (This was not my first brush with pain that day. I had been putting cigarettes out on my arm for a while.)

Chuck's right hand was the last thing I remember from that night. But when I woke up, punches from the UFC light heavyweight champion were the least of my concerns. My armpit was blazing. On fire. That made sense when I saw my brand-new armpit tattoo, "Back Flip Bitch." That's a nickname I gave Carey, in honor of him being the first moto rider to ever land a backflip in competition. We had been doing Tony's show at Carey's tattoo shop, Hart and Huntington, and I was a drunk blacked-out asshole, so it wasn't too difficult to connect the dots on that one.

But, like the pain from Chuck Liddell's punches, "Back Flip

Bitch" was also not my most pressing issue. That would have been my asshole, which was currently screaming with pain.

It's times like these when you're lucky to have friends. I called Hart immediately. I was nearly in tears. "Carey," I said. "What the fuck did I do last night?" That question alone should tell you something. I was prepared to believe I had done pretty much anything imaginable involving my ass. As it turns out, I had dared some girl to try to make me spill my beer by kicking me in the nuts. I'm told she tried that repeatedly. Only trouble is, her aim wasn't so good, plus she was wearing spiked heels, so I caught numerous errant shots in more of the taint and ass region.

Tony Hawk had a bachelor party right after that. That was the one time after the Chuck Liddell night that I got properly obliterated. That's when I finally bottomed out. While I was recovering from Tony's party, I was on a plane to Australia having these intense heart palpitations. I was positive I was having a heart attack. I was sure I was dying. I was scared absolutely shitless.

I'd had enough. I didn't want to die. Only one thing really kept me going through the years. It was this sense I had. This feeling that kept telling me, *I am not going to die as the shithead I am now. A thirty-three-year-old washed-up skater.*

A fucking loser.

PART FOUR

Credit: Ryan Steely

Hanging out on one of
my dad's friend's bikes.

Me at two with my mum.
The first of many
fucked-up bowl cuts.

With Santa at five.

On the way to a Kiss show with Lee, about six years old. My dad took me right up to the stage and Gene Simmons flicked blood on my shirt.

Doing a wheelie on a bike in Sandringham, about nine. This bike was my only friend until skateboarding came along.

On my dad's friend's boat on vacation in Sydney, at thirteen.

With Lee, barefoot waterskiing in the
Yarra River, about fourteen.

After my dad informed me that I was wasting everyone's time in school, I quit at the age of sixteen and he bought me this sweet outfit for my job as a supermarket trolley boy.

Sixteen years old and all dressed up for my mum's wedding day. She married a guy who once water-skied from Victoria to Tasmania.

Drinking Victoria Bitter beer at Misty's house, eighteen or nineteen years old.

At twenty-five, with Mom, when she quit drinking. Here I am celebrating the occasion with a beer.

With Tony Hawk and pro skater Buster Halterman, sometime in the mid 90s. If Tony's drinking Absinthe then this was in Prague.

During my first trip to the US. Lance Mountain took this picture of me for *Transworld* magazine. Big day. I thought I had finally arrived. Little did I know.

Credit: LanceMountain.com

Before there was the MegaRamp, DC had the super ramp.

Riding motocross.

The MegaRamp at Point X.
I landed the second ever
Kickflip Indy after Danny Way.

The Ellis brothers, fully strapped, at our vacation house in Tanjil Bren. [Left to right: Lee, Jason, and Stevie.]

Method Air, in Australia, 1996. Taken for a Pro Spotlight in *Transworld*. Getting featured was way up on the list of things I wanted to accomplish as a skateboader. That was a huge deal for me.

At a Tony Hawk demo. I wanna say in Kentucky. During one of my sober and fit phases, with Sara.

Guinness World Record drop in. And the plaque I got for it. Kind of lame, really. But the check was nice.

With Lee and Dad at dinner when Lee won Rookie of the Year in Aussie Motocross. They both had to give a speech that night. That's why they both look terrified. I'm the only talker in my family.

Grimey.

Beer bonging
with Colin McKay
and the crew on
Gigantic Skate
Park Tour bus.

With Danny Way
and Bucky Lasek
in England. We
got flown over to
do one demo. This
is one of the last
times I got paid to
be a skateboader.

Me and my good
buddy Carey Hart,
aka Twinkletoes.

Andrea and me, when we first met.

Our wedding, poolside at the Hard Rock in Las Vegas.

With Stevie (left) and Lee (middle), right after my father died.

From the music video for "Monkeys of War" by my band Taintstick, before we changed our name to Death! Death! Die!

Truck racing.

At the
Howard Stern Show.

With my bestie Benji Madden
(of Good Charlotte) performing
with Taintstick at Ellis Mania.

After my boxing match, at the Hard Rock Las
Vegas. [Left to right: Mayhem Miller, Ryan
Parsons, Justin Fortune, me, and Kit Cope.]

Dynamite in my hands! A first-round
knockout at my boxing match.

With Andrea and my daugther, Devin.

With Devin at the beach in Oceanside.

Introducing Devin to my favorite band.

With my brothers, Marn and Devin, after my dad died.

14.

HOLY SHIT,

I'VE GOT A BABY!

As terrifying as it was to think I was potentially about to die at thirty thousand feet, what made it even worse was that I was on the plane to Australia with my girlfriend, who had our unborn child in her belly.

Toward the end of my long drug-fueled haze, I had met Andrea. She was a friend of a guy that skated for DC. Actually, I'd met her before, at Colin McKay's house. She was there on a date. With Colin. She didn't sleep with him, but they made out. I've always made fun of them for that. This was way back when I had Grimey. During the height of my Paris

Hilton phase. I don't even remember. I probably showed up wasted, got more wasted, left to go somewhere else to get even more wasted than that, and that was the end of it.

I met her for the second time at a bar. I was thirty. She was twenty. She had gotten in with a fake ID. I was still on cocaine and had done a ridiculous amount that night. This was when I was no longer doing cocaine to be social. I don't know why I was doing it. Just addicted, I guess. It was the era where I would do so much coke, I preferred to just stay home with my cronies and do it around a table. I had become kind of a party pooper. As we were doing it, I'd be complaining, "We're losing the plot here, man. We're losing it!" As you might imagine, I was an awesome guy to hang out with.

But on this particular night, after doing tons of coke, I did leave the cocaine table to go to the local bar. I was very anxious to start drinking my double vodka tonics, to wear off the cocaine enough to get out there and start talking to some chicks. I had been on my own for a while. I had escaped from Sara. I was in America, single, and making some real money. Things were good, and I partied hard.

I went up to Andrea at this bar. She was with her friends. I said, "How's it going?" and put my arm around her. I believe that somebody at the bar had already told her that I was a skateboard dickhead. So I had a little bit going for me. But I was so shit hammered. Back then, though, I could be that wasted and still hold a conversation. Maybe even remember your name afterward, or something romantic like that.

I tried to make out with her. My old go-to move. I just leaned in and went for it. Like a gross wasted dude. That didn't fly. So then I just tried to talk to her, and said I liked her, and got her number. I tried to make her come home with me, and she wouldn't. Which would have been somebody else's house, anyway.

That night, I texted her that she should come by my friend's house and bring me a cheeseburger, because I was hungry. Then I got back to the couch and smoked the Mull-Bongs, the weed combined with American Spirit tobacco. Then I passed out.

I woke up in the morning with a cheeseburger on my back. I called her. I said, "I know you like me, because you brought me a cheeseburger."

MY SINGLE PHASE LASTED LESS than a year before I started seeing Andrea. But you could say she had good timing. She showed up on time for the "I wanna grow up" Jason. Although believe me, she still got put through it plenty. I had only recently gotten divorced, and I let Andrea know straight up that I was done with marriage for good. (Not that she saw me as husband material, I'm sure.) Because of what I'd been through, she was the first chick I ever leveled with. I had no reason to hide anything, so I didn't.

I told Andrea from the start: I'll sleep with anybody. I'll do cocaine all the time. I'll smoke weed in the middle of the night. (That wasn't an exaggeration, by the way—I would wake up and smoke weed, to go back to sleep.) I'll do ecstasy. I'll do anything, and I'll fuck anybody.

I didn't like myself. I had just given up. I thought I was scum. I thought I was disgusting. I had that opinion of myself. I got bummed out whenever I thought too deeply about myself. *Just be high,* I would tell myself. *Don't analyze yourself.* Which made it worse, because then, afterward, I would wake up with even more disgust from the drug hangover. Not to mention from the things I was doing while I was high. This had started a long time ago. I think that's what helped me get into heroin. Because I didn't care anymore. About me, anyway.

I was honest about who I was with Andrea. Right off the bat. But I said we could hang out. I think she saw that I had potential. I think a lot of girls are able to look at guys like that.

For a long while there, we were really just friends. But we did have a first date. She came by my house. Actually, because I had given Sara my house, I invited her over to Ken Block's house—the owner of DC. Ken wasn't even there. And she brought a friend. Obviously to cock-block, and be safe. But I guess Andrea gave the signal, because then the friend left, and we made out in this massive Jacuzzi with a rock wall, overlooking the ocean. This was the greatest house I'd ever been inside in my whole entire life. We had margaritas and chilled in the Jacuzzi.

She wouldn't sleep with me. It took like a week of dates. We were smoking pot and drinking. I kind of got her into smoking pot. We were just hanging out and playing video games. Moto. We would play together. Or sometimes, I would play, and she would just watch me and cheer me on. One time, she actually beat me, because she would practice as much as I did.

Because of all the mistakes I'd made in my life with women, I had a really low opinion about myself in relationships. Sara wasn't the right person for me, but at the time, I believed that I was a cunt, and that my antics alone had driven her insane. Which is an argument you could make, for sure. Even if she did handle it all like a psychopath.

And don't get me wrong—Sara *was* crazy. The first time Andrea ever saw her, Sara was beating me up in the middle of the street, while Andrea drove off to save herself. I had gotten my house in Vista back. Andrea would come over, but we would always worry about Sara. Sure enough, one time I heard the garage door open. I knew it was her, because she had refused to give me any keys back. So I scoot Andrea out the front door. As I'm getting her out of the house and in the car, Sara comes out of the garage. While Andrea gets away, Sara runs up to me on the street and starts wailing on me.

So maybe Sara was crazy without any of my help. But even if Sara hadn't already been crazy, I would have driven her insane. I would have done it to anybody. If you were really in love with me, and you were trying to have a relationship with me, I would have driven you insane.

Andrea and I started living together, in the house in Vista. And then I started paying for Andrea's car. I wanted to take care of her. I told her that maybe she didn't have to go to school. She could just live with me, and I'd pay for her. I really started to lean on her. Because that's how it goes with me: Somebody's got to take care of me, you know?

One time, later on when we had gotten more serious, someone texted me. Someone from back when I was on tour. And Andrea had my phone at that moment. I hadn't actually met this other girl, but I'd had text-sex with her. And it was in my phone. Andrea saw it all. When she saw it, she yelled at me. And I flinched. Covered my head, instinctively. She was like, "What are you doing?" Because the last time I got caught doing something like that, with Sara, hellfire had rained down on my face. But Andrea said, "I would never hit you. No matter what you do."

The wheels started turning, inside my brain. *You would never hit me? No matter what I do? So that means . . . you're still considering continuing to talk to me?* Because at that point, I was thinking, not only would we never talk to each other ever again, but she was gonna call her dad and have me stabbed or something. I felt like I was being real out of line, with someone who is a saint, and who is never going to retaliate and be the violent insane person that I'm used to dating.

Every serious relationship that I ever had, when it got rocky, my girlfriend would lash out and either hit me, or say things about me to other people that were beyond low blows. Rachel would say stuff to people about my mum, or about me being gay because I was molested. That one would get me. When I was younger, I thought maybe I *was* gay. Because I was raised in a world where, if the things that happened to me happened to you, you were a fag. It didn't have to make sense—that was the way it was. I'd had times where I'd been drinking, and I'd be saying, "I don't know if I'm gay. I don't know who I am." And Rachel would just work on that.

At first, Andrea was just a little girl when she was with me. And her background couldn't have been more different from where I was coming from. I think Andrea's parents raised her in a way that affected the way she saw me. I never went out with anybody in my whole life whose parents were like Andrea's. Easily the most normal people I have ever met. They say "I love you" to each other all the time. Unless a tree crashes on their house or something, to them, everything's going to be okay.

I remember meeting Andrea's mother. We went to a massage place or a facial place and Andrea's mom met us in the parking lot. I could tell it was a surprise and that Andrea hadn't planned that. I think the parents wanted to get a look at this guy that was seeing their daughter. I didn't want to meet them, because I'm older than Andrea and because I was on drugs all the time. But then her mother got in the car and said hello. It was very obvious she wanted to scope me out.

Other than that one ambush, I don't think I really met her parents properly for six months, at least. We were together for maybe a year before I would say it was a relationship. Although it probably really had been a relationship for a while before that. I don't think I admitted it because I wanted an excuse to cheat. I was also sleeping with some other girl, and we'd have fights about it. She told her parents, and that made them very, very angry at me. I would fuck anybody. The most hideous of people. I was just trying to fill the void. The vicious cycle of doing things that were going to make me feel bad in the morning. Instant gratification and then total regret and then do it all over again. I think Andrea saw that pattern and tried to intercept it.

We were having unprotected sex. I think Andrea was hoping she might get pregnant. I thought I might want to leave something on the planet to continue my name. And I thought fatherhood might make me grow up a little, too. Having a child wasn't exactly planned, but then again there was a time when I even told my dad, "You know, I think we may have a baby." I had no idea what the fuck I was saying, or doing. Although I did know that I was a serious person when it came to kids. And if a baby did ever come, I always thought that I could sober up and become a real father. I always thought that about myself. Fatherhood is a very serious job. Even back when I was out of my mind, if someone had said, "Hey, I'm pregnant," I would've at *least* said, "Okay, I'm gonna be shitfaced, but here, you can have all my money."

When we found out Andrea was pregnant, I remember saying, "Well, we've got money, and I'll be there for you. You know as well as I do that you'll be doing the parenting. Don't expect this to be some sort of Cinderella story. But I'll do the best I can with the things I have to offer."

Me and Andrea is the longest relationship I've ever been in. My relationships all followed the same pattern—it wasn't gonna work, and I knew it, but I stayed because I'm fucking terrified of breaking up with anybody. Six years is usually the breaking point. That's when I finally say I can't fucking do it anymore. That's when things got rocky with Rachel.

But after three years with Andrea, our daughter, Devin, was born. I announced it to the world on Tony Hawk's radio show, right from the hospital. Devin changed everything. I wanted to break up with Andrea a million times. I don't understand how Andrea stayed with me, either. But for the sake of Devin's life we just kept going. That's definitely what kept us together. A lot of times, Andrea wouldn't have taken my shit. She would have been long gone. But it's not fair to the child to just give up. So we did everything in our power to stay together so that the kids don't have to go through what I've gone through. I think Andrea has seen, through me, what weird parenting can do to a child. I think the way things were when I was a kid made me a little bit crazy.

Many times, I've been in way over my head as a father. Even doing basic stuff. One time, I tried to take Devin for a walk in her stroller, while walking my dog, Fifty, at the same time. And I couldn't pull it off. Devin was crying, and Fifty was getting tangled on stuff. I had to take Fifty back to the house and walk Devin by herself. I literally could not walk a dog and a child at the same time. Being a parent is hard. In a lot of ways.

I think, like a lot guys, having a daughter instantly changed my opinion of women. It made me respect and appreciate girls more. Beyond that, for Devin's sake—and for my son, Tiger, too, when he was born a few years later—being a dad made me committed to never giving in. There's a part of me that could go permanently dark. Forever. But not anymore. It's not an option. Not when you have kids. I need to be around them, and protect them. I want them to be glad I am their father. They're going to be loved. A lot of things people need to learn for themselves. But as much as you can learn about life from your parents, I want to be there to teach them those lessons.

I remember seeing Devin's red hair, and it hit me: she was an

Ellis. Tiger, too. I've always been very proud of the blood in my veins. I feel like members of the Ellis family have a lot of potential. I think my father was a talented person, and he passed that down to me, and I passed that down to my children. My kids will have a lot of opportunities, because they won't have the same kinds of scars that I got.

Me and Andrea got married after Devin was born, at the Hard Rock in Las Vegas. And then I just made myself be there for her. It wasn't love at first sight for us. It never has been for me. It was always lust. It's always, "You're hot. I'm in love with you. Let's date and be serious for the rest of our lives. Now none of you assholes look at her." When Andrea first got pregnant, I did not necessarily think that I was going to be with her for the rest of my life. It was more, "Now I'm gonna take care of this *kid* for the rest of my life." I figured, at least, that Andrea was the most together girl I've ever dated, so when we broke up, she wouldn't tell Devin that her father is an asshole and a whore and a drug addict.

My mum didn't do that. She told me my dad is this and my dad is that. "He drives fast with you in the car. It just goes to show how irresponsible he is." I knew that Andrea would not be that person. I remember thinking that—at least she won't talk shit on me.

Andrea got pregnant around the beginning of my red wine phase. Red wine and painkillers and weed. Part of that started with my moto accidents. I was trying to jump this triple, which was incredibly stupid. I was nowhere near good enough. I saw someone else do it—a pro, Mike LaRocco—and I was there on my 250 2-stroke, and I just went for it. I went sideways in the air, clipped the landing, and then my face collided with the next jump on the course.

My arms were crossed in front of me. I broke both of my elbows and separated my shoulder. I had the full-on double sling thing. I was basically mummified. I was on painkillers for three straight months. And then when it healed three months later, I went for the exact same jump and did the exact same thing: rebroke both my elbows, dislocated my other shoulder, and got swollen intestines. I honestly didn't go back with the intention of trying the jump again. I didn't even tell anyone I was about to do it. I just got lost in the moment. The bottom line with me is: if I'm not being supervised, look out.

I got a CAT scan and had to drink that fluorescent drink. Then I did three more months on painkillers. Not that I minded, at the time. I was just numbing myself. Sedation. I was really fat then too, for me. Blobbing out. I would get the munchies like crazy at night. To the point where I would feel bad. I remember getting ice cream bars and eating them in my bathroom, so Andrea didn't see me. Not that she would've said anything—just that I had already started to frown on my own habits. What I had become.

Tony Hawk's bachelor party was right after my double moto accidents, and it was the beginning of the end of me drinking. The end of a lot of stuff. I came home wasted from the party, and Andrea was pissed at me. She told me I had to stop drinking, and I said I would try. I said that so many times.

Then we got on the plane to Australia. Devin was in Andrea's stomach. And I convinced Andrea to let me have a glass of red wine. I fell asleep and when I woke up, my heart was going off. I felt this fear. I was going to die. That was it. I was sure. Right then and there. Any second now.

When we landed, somebody gave me a Valium and it calmed me down. But as far as I was concerned, I had had a heart attack on the plane. Nobody knew. Even Andrea didn't get the severity of it. When we got there, she asked if I was feeling better. I said I was, and that was the end of it, for then.

We were in Australia for Christmas. There was a party. Stevie and Lee came over to my mum's house. Stevie was like, "You're not having a beer?" I told him I didn't want one. And I wasn't lying.

I remember talking to my dad, in the garden on the side of the house.

"You're happy?" he asked me. I told him I was. "I'm happy." And he looked at me. "You're gonna get fat when you get older." I think he was trying to hint that I already *was* fat.

I had already quit drinking a million times before. But it was different this time. I had a child on the way. I had just started a new career on the radio. That glass of red on the plane wasn't the last drink I ever had. But it was the beginning of the end, for sure. I couldn't just get wasted and not worry about it. The fear had been put in me.

Whatever the hell happened to me on that flight to Australia, I finally believed that drinking and drugs were going to kill me.

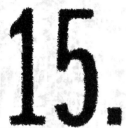

15.

BAD TIMES

From my early days on radio, I truly believed that I would become a gigantic star. But there was no way of knowing for sure. And it wasn't that much of a paycheck, either. So when Andrea was pregnant with Devin, for better or for worse, I was still just a skater.

At that point, there was only one MegaRamp at Point X, a skate and BMX camp in Southern California. We were all skating it. I was still maybe a top ten vert guy, but I wasn't really that good anymore. Not as good as I used to be. No way. So when the MegaRamp came along, I went there as much as I could. It was make or break time.

I had done a couple of tricks there that no one else had done. I was kind of hanging with everybody again. Tail Grab Frontside 360s into Kickflip Indies on the quarter pipe. Which was pretty big. I kind of had that down. And there were probably only ten of us that could jump that thing in the first place. So that was kind of a banger. I was maybe top five on the MegaRamp. And then I learned Indie 360 over the gap. I was trying them one day. I remember Bob Burnquist was there, and Jake Brown, and maybe Bucky Lasek.

So I roll in. I do the Indie 360. I remember I was a little off balance, but I was like, *I'm making this for sure.* No matter what. And I remember letting go early and just spinning around without my hands on the board. I was like, *Wow, I could probably do this without even grabbing.* I had really good control.

I landed after the gap, and heading for the quarter pipe I thought, *I just did an Indie 360, it's only natural to do an Indie 540.* I never even tried one on the MegaRamp before. And when I do Indie 540s, I flip, I don't spin. It looks like a front flip, kind of. I'm exactly upside down at one point.

So I flip upside down, and I look over my shoulder, and right as I grab my board, I know that I'm way off, over the deck. I can't see it, but you can just sense it. As soon as I grabbed my board, I knew it was trouble. I was probably about sixteen feet above the coping. Fuck. The first thing I did was kick my board away from me. I stopped my spin, from the panic.

Another skater, Brian Patch, landed feet first on the MegaRamp, and he got a spinal fracture. Up his foot, through his leg, to his back, and he didn't skate for like a year. It shattered whatever he had landed on, and everything attached to it.

But I'm upside down. I'm not getting anywhere *near* my feet. On the MegaRamp, there's so much time in the air to see what's happening. It fucks with you. If you have a car crash, you don't see it coming.

Somehow that's not so bad. But if you have two full seconds to see the slam coming, that's bad. I was so high up in the air. I've done this slam before, but not from sixteen feet. I did it before at eight feet, and it almost broke my fucking back.

So I'm thinking: *This could be it.*

WHAM! I landed on my hip. Hard. I'm on autopilot. Almost in shock. The ramp bounced me out, and my feet started to go over my head. I remember making the decision to tuck and hold on to my knees, to flip around again, because otherwise I'm gonna land with all my weight on my face and snap my head backward. Probably break my neck. The ramp is like eighteen feet high, so now that I've already slammed into the coping, I'm about to fall another eighteen feet, straight onto my chin. For the second time I think: *This might be my last moment of life.*

I flip over and land on my back. *BOOM!* Nothing moved. It paralyzed my legs. I couldn't feel them. I figured that if I couldn't feel my legs, I must have broken my back.

I remember Jake Brown coming over. I've known Jake ever since he was sixteen, when he tried to sell me weed at a skate ramp in Australia. Check that—when he *sold* me weed at a skate ramp. He looked sad. I was like, "Fuck off." We both tried to laugh, as the feeling started coming back into my legs. Pretty much immediately we started joking about it, blowing it off a little, but this was a real deal slam. I still have a piece of my ass missing.

That hit rag-dolled me so hard, I feel like if I hadn't landed right on my hip, a little lower or a little higher, it would have ripped something off. It was a death hit. At that speed, it was like a motorcycle accident, where you pop some organs.

I didn't go to the hospital though. At least not right away. Andrea drove me home. Back then I already had plenty of painkillers without going to see a doctor. And plenty of red wine as well.

This was before Jake's famous slam at the X Games in 2007. This was one of the first big slams on the MegaRamp. Three other skaters have done what I did—crashed on the coping—and people still watch the videos of all three, just because of what horrific slams they are. Jake is the only one who did the other slam, where you fall all the way down to the flat. No one will even let themselves get close to having that happen to them, because they'll die. I still don't understand how Jake lived.

My fall freaked me out. After predicting the end of my career since before it even really started, this was the end. I started to feel this fear. I wouldn't admit it. But I started to rationalize not committing to stuff. I probably still haven't admitted it. Here it is: I was scared. Too scared to be on the MegaRamp. Too scared to compete with those dudes. Too scared to skate anymore, period. My confidence was shot. There were a lot of heavy things happening around then. Matt Hoffman, the greatest BMX rider who ever lived, had permanent brain damage. I became a poser. I just lost it. I was never committed to landing anything anymore. I had accepted a long time ago that I wasn't going to become the greatest skateboarder on earth. So was I really going to *die* for this?

I had reached a real low point in my life. I had seen the end coming with skateboarding, but now I was responsible for more than myself. For several years, I had been in denial about the risks I took on a skateboard. But it was time to cut the shit. Andrea was pregnant with Devin. Forget about me—I needed to support *them*.

And it got worse. Andrea was going through the mail one day and she found a letter. I never even checked the mail. She was reading it, telling me I might be fucked. It turned out no one had paid my taxes for five years. "That's bullshit," I said. "My agent and his people handle everything."

My old agent used to get my checks and pay all my bills. I just had an ATM card. I would call and say "I need a car" or "I need a hotel room" and they'd just get it for me. They paid my phone bill. Occasionally they would tell me to slow down on spending for a week, here and there, but that was as much as I was involved in my financial planning. I could blame them, but it's my fault, for being a massive baby and not handling my shit. Still, it was devastating. I sold my house, and I was still $200,000 short on what I owed the government. That was when my income was really thin, too. I had a lot of good stories from skateboarding, but I officially had no money to show for it whatsoever.

ON NEW YEAR'S EVE, ANDREA and me stayed home. It was a quiet night. Because she was pregnant, there was no drinking. Maybe I smoked a little weed, but that was it. The next morning—New Year's Day 2005—Lee called me from Australia.

"Dad's gone."

I didn't even know what he meant. He was crying. I've never seen Lee cry. It made no sense to me at all. And then somebody—I think it was Marn—got on the phone. "He's had a heart attack, pedaling up Tanjil this morning."

It just didn't make any sense. "He's dead or he's not dead?" I asked. "I don't understand what the fuck you people are saying." I gave the phone to Andrea. I had that feeling again—the same one from the plane ride—the feeling of my heart jumping out of my chest. A panic attack, I guess. Although I didn't know what a panic attack even was.

Me and my dad didn't talk much on the phone. Ever. The last time we ever talked one-on-one was the time in Australia when he told me I was fat. But he had left a message for New Year's.

I went back to Australia. I saw him, in the casket. I wrote a letter and put it in there with him. I said I was sorry for making his life so much harder. First I couldn't get good grades in school, and then my solution was to become a fucking skateboarder? Really? Getting into fights with his wife? I apologized for bringing him so much unnecessary drama.

My dad was gone. This was beyond shocking. I was an Ellis. I believed that we were invincible.

My dad was not a cyclist in any way. By all accounts, it was a spur of the moment decision. I wasn't there, but I can tell you that he must have pedaled like hell the whole way, because that's the way he did everything. Just like me. All in. Right up to when it gave him the heart attack. It wasn't even his bike. It was Lee's bike. Lee has pedaled up this mountain, and he said it was the hardest thing he ever did in his life. Lee is a top ten motocross guy in Australia, who runs and pedals every day. He runs six miles every morning. And my dad has never run anywhere. Sure, maybe he rides moto and chain saws shit. But my father didn't do cardio. He's never jogged. He doesn't go to the gym. He's got a dumbbell in the backyard. That's his gym.

I know exactly what he was thinking. *Wait until I get back and tell Lee what a pussy he is.* It was that simple. He had done tons of crazy, stupid stuff his whole life. He thought he had the heart of a young man, and he didn't anymore. Most people would have stopped, but he just kept going.

He never really changed, right up to the end. When Andrea and I were in Australia, back when we started dating, we had one of these vintage all-nighters. One of those times where a big group of people were drinking everything we could get our hands on, in order to get as ludicrously shitfaced as possible.

This was the last time we really raged together, before he died.

It was the New Year's before, and everyone was playing some kind of drinking game. We'd been playing for like an hour when Dad got involved. Whatever the game was, he kept losing and losing and losing. And we were drinking all kinds of fucked-up stuff—Jack and tequila and vodka. The object of the game was definitely not to enjoy what you were swigging down your throat. We drank so much alcohol it was ridiculous. Especially my dad.

And then at one point someone had a heat gun out. This thing that peels paint. It's got this little donut hole on the end, and fire shoots out of it. Always good to have one of these around when you're drinking. My dad had just bought it the other day, and he's showing it off. My little brother's friend is right there. "Fuck, that'd burn you pretty good, wouldn't it, Steve?" he says. My dad flicked it toward him, but Dad was drunk, so he accidentally burned the dude pretty good. The kid freaks out and lets out a pretty good yell. "Come on," my old man says. "It didn't hurt that bad."

The guy shows my dad the burn on his arm, and my dad holds his ground. "That ain't that bad," he says. "Lookit." And then my father puts the heat gun on his own arm and turns it on. And he holds it there.

"AHH! AHHHH!" Clearly he's in the midst of intense pain. He's yelling. But he keeps it there. Because he's showing you how long he can do it. A bubble forms, and rises, and then pops. A SKIN bubble. And then ANOTHER one rises and pops. That's how long he held it there. "*AHHHHH!!!*"

There's maybe twenty people there. We're all hammered. Other than him, we're all young. We're all idiots. The night before, we'd all been branding each other. Stevie's friend had gotten the letter E branded on each ass cheek. This was *not* an Ellis. The guy's name is Tom fucking Payton. There is no E in his name whatsoever. So we are not a responsible crowd. People are falling over, smashing shit, opening gashes that technically require stitches, but fuck, the hospital's too far away, so put a Band-Aid on it and bleed, motherfucker. No one is showering. This is a diesel weekend. But nonetheless, the crowd is taken aback by this display. "Steve, you've gone too far!"

My father was impressed with his handiwork. "Fucking hell, look at that," he says. So we laugh. And so he laughs. "Fuck, that hurt," he says. We keep drinking. We keep hanging out. That was really just a few seconds out of the night. He was arm-wrestling not long after attempting to fire blast that same arm off his body. And I think he won. We moved on to throwing knives at each other, I believe. People are bleeding everywhere. This was a big night. We had snorted all the drugs and moved on to what was left, crushing up aspirins and beer-bonging schnapps. We were just lost.

Dad didn't do cocaine or ecstasy or anything like that, so he passed out around three, I imagine, as us youngsters raged onward. When he woke up the next morning, the arm was hurting, but he went to work. He tried to ride it out. A couple days later, it was *really* hurting, so he went to the doctor. It was bleeding and oozing, and it turned out he was getting gangrene. They told him he was lucky he came in when he did, because he could have lost the arm.

He was my boy. He was a legend to me and my brothers, and to all our friends. Because he would go further than anyone. I've got so much video footage of him chopping trees down and almost having the tree fall down on top of him. One second he's got the chain saw, and the next second he's running for his life and diving at the last second as the tree explodes on the ground right next to him. Then popping back up. "I'm all right! One of the branches got me in the back pretty good. No biggie."

My dad was always my idol. The standard I held myself up

against. He was also the one person on earth I really felt I could count on if the shit went down. I remember, when I lived in that cocaine dealer's house in California, back when I was still on the Bones Brigade, I took some mushrooms—the ones that are in chocolates. Which is totally cheating, by the way. Too easy. But anyway, they kicked in, and I didn't like it. I didn't want to be there. I wanted it to stop. I was watching TV, and simultaneously figuring out an emergency plan. I decided that if the mushrooms wouldn't go away, I could call Dad, and he could get there within a day. And that I could make it one day, until he got there. It's so crazy that after all those years, the second I felt like I was in actual, real danger, the first thing I thought was that he was the one person who could save me.

But as I had slowly dealt with the fact that I didn't want to be wasted all the time, I had felt my opinion about my dad starting to change, too. All the things that I'd been bottling up since I was a kid—like, how could my parents leave me alone with the kind of babysitter that would molest their child?—those things wouldn't stay bottled up anymore.

And now, as I was maybe ready to start confronting all that, out of nowhere my father was gone.

I remember drinking at the funeral, in Australia, with my friends. My dad was such a tough dude and had lived such a tough life, I don't think people thought that him dying was really that sad. "Well, you still got the Ellis brothers," they said. I felt like it hit me harder than it did everybody else. Me and Stevie. I think the two of us bonded because it was the hardest for us. Dad had been through so many things with Lee. He'd been disrespectful to Lee's wife, for one thing. I'm not saying everybody didn't love everybody, but I think I held my dad up higher than everybody else did. I still looked up to him. I had my problems with him, but I still idolized him at that point.

There are probably things about my dad I'll never know. I'm still finding out new shit, to this day. Like how, apparently, right before he passed away, he had purchased a house somewhere on the other side of town as a place to grow and sell hydroponic weed. He bought it, and some drug dealer dude lived there, selling the product. He was making tons of money—like thirty grand a month—for three months before the feds started catching on to them. They managed to shut down before the heat came down on them, and he died soon afterward, so that was the end of that.

Lee told me. I'd had no idea. Both of us sat there and wondered, "So what the fuck else did he do?" I'm not even sure I should be writing this book about me—one about him would be way better.

I had all these regrets. Not seeing my dad. Not being around. Being all about myself. I came to America to try to be a pro skateboarder, and now I've missed out on my father. If I had been around, maybe I could've stopped it. Maybe I could've helped him. Maybe I could've been there that morning, to say "What the fuck are you thinking?" Maybe I could've been awake at the same time and told him not to do it.

Dad's death was such a massive shock. It changed everything. I remember thinking nothing was ever going to be okay, ever again. For a long while there, everything was always sad. Devin's red hair. Just like my dad. Everything was a reminder that he wasn't gonna be around anymore.

I can't imagine what all this was like for Andrea. Falling in love with me, so far, had been like: "Okay, there's a drug addict here. Let's get him off the cocaine. Okay, there is also a massive drinking problem here. Let's try to get rid of that. Okay, now I'm pregnant. And now his father died. And wait a minute—you're telling me you're not that great of a skateboarder anymore? And that your agent didn't pay your taxes for five years? And that the house we live in is no longer ours? And you also owe $200,000?"

ABOUT A YEAR AFTER MY dad passed away, I took a break from being on the radio and went back to Australia on a DC Tour. We were at my old ramp. There was a really high wall there, with two ledges on it. I had always talked about jumping off it, onto the ramp. My old buddy Gregsy—Greg Stewart—called me up. "Are you gonna do it?" I told him I was. He was pumped.

No one on the DC team knew it. I was there as the announcer. But I was going to steal this demo. This was my home ramp. My homecoming. After the MegaRamp slam, I'd gotten really sketchy about pushing it and getting hurt. I was done with courting danger on a regular basis. But this was my good-bye to skateboarding. Back where it all started.

There was a new ramp there. It wasn't *my ramp* anymore. It was really slippery. I hated it. I warmed up a little bit, but I couldn't get anything going. *Fuck warm-ups,* I thought. *I'm just gonna go for it.*

So I climbed up the ramp and over the rail and I went all the way up to the roof. And then I look over. I was maybe forty feet off the ground, looking down on a fourteen-foot ramp. What I was about to attempt was borderline humanly impossible. I had maybe a 5 percent chance of sticking it, the way I saw it. *Fuck,* I thought. *I'm about to die.*

Everyone looked up at me. They all started cheering. I knew I could jump in and knee slide down the ramp. I figured that would "Ooh! Ahh!" a couple of people, so I did that a couple times. But after I did that, that's when I started to believe I could pull it off.

I gave myself a pep talk. This was my last chance of ever doing something cool. No one had ever done this before. No one else will ever try it again. I'll go down in history. People will point at this wall for generations to come, and say, "Ellis jumped off that."

That was enough motivation to make me go for it, over and over again. I dropped in maybe eight times. And every time, I bailed on the landing.

Fuck it, I thought. *I'm gonna stick this one.* I was so committed, I dropped in with both feet on the board, and both hands. Dive bomb.

At the last second, I knew I was too far off the wall. Shit. I took my feet off right before impact. My knees were on the board when the board touched the ramp, and the board flipped me right off. My head hit the ramp, and I skidded down in the fetal position. I had a seizure. I pissed my pants. I was out. They carried me off and put me in an ambulance. I don't remember anything.

I woke up in the hospital, and they told me if I hit my head again I was gonna die.

From there we continued on to Mexico City. It was the worst trip ever. They had a MegaRamp there. It was a really high altitude, so you were going huge—like it or not. And I did a twenty-foot Backside air, the whole time thinking that if I hit my head I was dead.

That was the most dangerous thing I've ever done on a skateboard. But it was also the *greatest* thing I've ever done on a skateboard. Especially considering how old and washed up I was at that point. No one could give a shit but me. Bob Burnquist and Danny Way and Pierre-Luc Gagnon were there, and they were all better than me that day. But I don't care. I did a twenty-foot Backside air. Going huge like that is all I've ever wanted to do. Little skateboarder me back in Sandringham would have been so proud.

When I started out, all I wanted was one legendary contest ride. I never got it. The best ride I ever did, my friend Eddie Martin saw me do it, by ourselves, at Prahran Ramp. I did like an eight-foot Frontside Ollie and I did a 360 Body Jar out of a Boardslide to Fakie that was maybe six feet high. I've never seen anybody do a six-foot 360 Body Jar, ever. When nobody cared, and skateboarding had taken a shit, and I was on Prahran Ramp in Australia, that was the best I ever was. And all I got for it was a 10 percent discount on grip tape at Snake Pit.

Fuck it.

WHEN I WAS BACK IN Australia, I gave my brother Stevie my Red Dragons chain. My father dying had made me pull closer to him. I felt like his life could go in a lot of different directions. Stevie was drinking too much when my dad died. The chain blew his mind. It was worth like five grand. He was twenty-three when I gave it to him. He loved the Red Dragons.

"It's mine, but you can borrow it," I said. "I'll be back in a year. If you mess it up, or if you lose it, when I get back, you're fucked. If you get too drunk, you know you're gonna break it, or someone's gonna steal it." Where we're from, that chain is asking for trouble. If you're drunk, and you're being a smart-ass, someone will take it off you, just for being a smart-ass. In a weird way, the chain was my way of keeping an eye on him until I got back.

My life was finally starting to come together—the radio thing was going pretty good, I had finally stopped getting wasted—and I wanted Stevie to come along with me. I had been working on him. He quit smoking cigarettes. He quit drinking so much. He was growing out his hair. I told him to. "One day you won't have hair," I said. "Trust me. Look at me."

So I got him sobered up. I called him as often as I could. I was heading to Australia to see him again. And then one night, he gets drunk with all his friends. And they do a bunch of coke, and the next day, none of them have slept. That's all they ever did. Drinking and driving and stupid shit. So they've been up all night, and at seven o'clock in the morning, they decide to go get more beer. They drive down the mountain, get the beer, and on the way back up, they see a steamroller on the side of the mountain.

They decide to hot-wire it. Among Stevie's friends, he was the daredevil. So he's the first one on it. The first one to drive it. Rolling over traffic signs. He was trying to roll over a steel pole, but the pole didn't snap. It bent a little instead, and the fucking steamroller went off the cliff. Stevie fell out. The thing rolled over him and killed him instantly.

Dead.

Twenty-four.

Done.

Gone.

Unlike with my dad, Stevie's was a sober funeral. We were all sober. I got the Red Dragons chain back. My ex, Rachel, showed up. I don't know why. She didn't know my brother. But I didn't get angry. I was trying to love everybody, because otherwise I thought I might kill someone.

Looking at that crowd, all I could think was that Stevie wouldn't be dead if everybody there wasn't so fucking stupid. If I had let myself get drunk, I would have started taking people out. "Fuck, mate, at least he had a good fucking dinner before he died." Somebody told me that, as their condolences.

I tried to understand it all. I took one of Stevie's friend's outside and asked him what had happened. I could tell I was making him nervous.

"Stevie was driving," the guy said. "We went down there after he fell. There was a little bit of blood coming out of his mouth. We tried to resuscitate him. But he was gone." I found out the next day that this was the guy that had wanted to go to the bottle shop. They'd been awake for two days, and this guy wanted to get more beer.

Lee wanted to kill him. "It's not his fault," I said. "He loved Stevie. He's just a fucking idiot. We've all done stupid shit." I wouldn't have minded if Lee had given him a soccer kick, though.

None of us will ever see him again. My stepmum's life is ruined. My brother's life is ruined. I'll never be the same.

Stevie didn't have the one thing that I had—my passion for skateboarding. I broke off that raging lifestyle, at least for a while, in my teens, because I had a passion. When I first fell in love with being a skateboarder, I didn't drink. I didn't do any drugs. I shaved my head. I went to the ramp every day. I didn't have any friends. I didn't talk to anyone. I didn't fuck chicks. I had no fucking life. Skateboarding took over, and my confidence in being a skateboarder gave me confidence as a human being. People who partied looked like losers to me. And I was right.

Unlike me at his age, Stevie had good friends. He had a way better life than I did in my teens and early twenties. He had a lot of fun. His mum would let him get away with all kinds of shit. His life was never like my life. He was raised the easy way.

In our town, I'm a famous guy. Not a massive big deal, but still. And then his older brother Lee became the number one supercross guy in Victoria. Number four in Australia. "Your brother's Jason Ellis? And your other brother's Lee Ellis?" He must have heard that a million times. So what's he gonna be?

He tried snowboarding, but he gave up on that. He tried to shine in other ways. When he'd get drunk, he was always the guy that was jumping off stuff. He would always push it. He would always go too far. "Ellis is crazy." The first time I heard that, it took me a second to realize they were talking about my brother, and not me.

That's why you've got to do something with your life. I knew my brother was in trouble the day my dad let him sell his snowboard to buy video games. I knew it. I tried to stop him. He got picked for the Australian snowboard team. They flew him to Aspen to compete, when he was like fifteen. He was good. But then my dad told me Stevie was selling his snowboard to get an Xbox.

The crowd he ran with, those guys would do ecstasy and coke all weekend and then work all week to save the money to do it all over again the next weekend. They party all night Friday night, straight through Saturday and Saturday night, and then they sleep enough on Sunday to go to work on Monday. That's what people do when they don't have a direction or a passion in their life. And then sooner or later they fuck up, get a chick pregnant, and then they try to grow up and deal with that. That's what the forgotten children of the world do. Your average suburbanite who isn't born rich or supersmart. A guy who will maybe learn a trade, but he won't like his job. He'll be angry about it. He'll get wasted to block it out, make bad decisions. And with a little bad luck, maybe even go to jail. Or you've been doing OxyContins every weekend, and so someone gives you some heroin, and at that moment it doesn't seem like that bad of an idea, so you stick a needle in your arm. One thing leads to another, and you die. It's that easy.

THE INSANITY MY DAD HAD rubbed off on me, and then I rubbed it off on Stevie. There was already a love/hate thing with my dad growing inside of me. But Stevie dying put it over the top.

I thought of a time, a few years earlier, when I'd been hanging out with Stevie and his friends. Right before I married Sara.

We were all watching a video in the living room. We'd shot it the night before. I've got a semiautomatic .22 in my hand, with like a twenty-five-shot magazine coming out of it. We were out spotlighting, in a truck, trying to shoot rabbits. It was like 2:00 A.M. Shitfaced. All of us. Someone hit the brakes and I went over the roof rack, down off the side of the car. I landed on my back with my hand in the air, holding the gun up. My brother's holding the camera, and it's on my face, with my eyes rolling back in my head. Really wasted. Stevie was ten years younger, so he would have been a teenager. That was a bad look, no doubt.

My dad walked in and saw the tape. "You're fucking joking me, Jay. Look at your fucking face there. Come on—that's fucking ridiculous. I told you a million times, don't be shitfaced with weapons."

But that was the end of it. He might have been dirty on me for a couple of hours, but it wasn't like he tried to ban me from touching guns, or from drinking. I could have had a beer right there, and it wouldn't have been an issue.

And besides, it wasn't like Dad hadn't fired guns wasted a thousand times. One time, we were all drunk, down by the Macalister River, and we lost a Bruno 270, which was a high-powered gun. And we went back another day to find the gun, with scuba gear, and everyone was drinking again. We had a rope tied to Dad, and he would go into the rapids in the scuba gear. And then he found it, pulled his gear off, grabbed some bullets, and started firing them off on the side of the river. The gun had been in the water for a couple weeks at that point. It could have blown up in his face.

My stepmother and even my mother had always tried to stop me from glorifying Dad's actions. "You guys don't know shit," I said.

"My dad is the coolest." I told my mum she was just jealous because he didn't want to go out with her anymore. Which was true. But she also had a point. Kids imitate everything their parents do. So there are two options: Did Dad not know that? Or did he not care? I don't have the answer. Both are plausible. If he was here, and he said he really didn't know, I would believe him. Or if he said he knew, but he still figured we'd be all right, I would believe that. It's probably a combination of both.

My dad and I are very similar. I think I can relate to him. And if I was stuck working for the family business, Ellistronics, I wouldn't be very satisfied either. For who he was, he should've left a million times. When I think about it now, and the things I know about him, and his sexual appetites, I see how hard it was for him to stick with us. Because he didn't want to. That wasn't him. He was a rogue. He was a maniac. He would've been way happier with a beard and a Harley-Davidson, fucking random stupid chicks out on the open road. He was very dedicated to the family. He tried.

One thing I learned about myself through all this is that I do move on. I just kept going. Life isn't fair. People die all the time that don't deserve to die. And plenty of people are alive who don't deserve to live. That doesn't give you the right to do drugs and throw your life away.

Harden the fuck up.

16.

RADIO OVERLORD

I was never a radio guy. And I'm not talking about being on the radio—I mean even just listening. All the time I spent in America, I never had a driver's license. I didn't have registration. I was a tourist. You could always find a way to buy some piece of shit car for like $800 and then drive that around. But they never had a radio or anything like that.

When I lived in that house I bought with Sara, in Vista, I started listening to Howard Stern in the mornings. I remember getting a shower radio just so I could listen, because every now and then he would say something that would make me laugh. It triggered something in me, and I liked the idea that he was helping me start my day. It felt like a special gift, for him to be able to do that for people. His show actually made my day a little bit better. It made me a little bit happier about my shit.

Then I saw *Private Parts,* and I was like, man, radio is fucking cool. I wouldn't say it immediately made me want to be in radio. It's maybe more like seeing a drummer in a cool metal band. You don't necessarily go out and buy a drum kit the next day, but you recognize that guy has a sweet job. *Private Parts* definitely made me think that being a radio host was a good gig. Even though, at that point, Stern was the only radio guy I knew, until I worked on the radio myself.

I did say, before I got into Stern, that I did fancy myself as a guy that could one day potentially retire and be on the radio. For some reason I had that in my head. I could always talk, and so possibly that would be the skill I would fall back on when athletically my body could no longer get me paid. But that wasn't a plan I had ever attempted to pursue or anything. It was just talk.

And then literally out of nowhere Tony Hawk called me in 2004 and said, "Hey, man, I have a radio show on this thing called Sirius." Of course, I had no idea what the fuck he was talking about. "I want you to be my cohost," he said. "Like, the funny guy. Jesse Fritsch"—a pro skater—"is the music guy, I'll be Tony Hawk, and you'll be the comedian." I was like, "Wow, cool, thanks for even thinking I'm a funny guy." It was really flattering that Tony would even think of me.

I still didn't really think anything of it, to be honest. But I remember getting in the studio, and as soon as I started talking, I felt like I had a gift. That was my first time ever on radio, on Tony's show. But as soon as that show started, I felt like I was way better at this than everybody in the room. That wasn't saying much, but at the time, it was still like, *Well, for starters, nobody else is better than me in here.* I've been waiting my whole life to find something I was naturally good at. I've never done anything where I was like, *Man, I was just born to do this.*

A long time ago, I had a conversation with a professional photographer, Dan Sturt, a crazy guy who base-jumped and did weird shit like that. I was hurt one day, and I was hanging out at the office of one of my sponsors. Dan was there to shoot an ad. And he said, "You don't actually think you were born to do this, do you?" I was like, "What do you mean?" "Skateboarding," he said. "You don't think you are actually *born* to be a skateboarder?" I told him yes, I *did* think that. "You think you've actually stumbled onto the one thing that you were born to do? Think about that. What are the odds? I guarantee you this is not what you were born to do, and there are one million things out there that you would be naturally better at." I was seventeen when he said that. I was like, "Why are you so fucking annoying?" But ever since then, that idea has been stuck in the back of my head.

Well, I feel like radio has been, so far, in my life, that thing that made me think, *Man, if I commit myself to this like I did to skateboarding, I could be the Tony Hawk of radio.* I thought I was born to be a skateboarder, and that was over. But now, maybe I *wasn't* born to be a skateboarder. Maybe I was born to be something bigger.

I couldn't piss away another chance.

Tony put me on his show, and I don't mind telling you—just like way back in Australia, that one day with Gary Valentine when I learned all those new tricks at once—almost instantly, it was obvious I was a potential future radio god.

We did our first segment on our first show, then took a break for a song. I don't even know what we were talking about. But one of the bosses came in, looked at me, and said, "Feel free to turn it up a bit."

Turn it up? Turn *what* up? I've been in radio for seven minutes! But that's what I did. I turned it up and found out that I could be instantly hilarious, and I could turn it off and turn it on. Nowadays I actually know what I'm doing on the radio, but for a long while there, I was just along for the ride. Stuff would just come out—I was an innocent bystander. I would hear what I said, along with everyone listening, and be like, *Wow. Way to go, dude!*

That moment, during Tony's first show, I decided to become the biggest radio host in the world. I really believed from the very start that I was gonna be the next big radio guy, and a massive millionaire. My stupidity fueled me. It's an amazing bullshit bubble I built in my brain to allow me to stay in the game and keep taking shit from radio bosses. *One day you will all see,* I told myself. *Mark my words.* Just living in a fantasy world.

Of course, I didn't say that out loud right away. Who would have listened to me? All I knew was, apparently Howard Stern was the best guy in radio, and Opie and Anthony were the best guys after him, and I was like, *I can beat those guys. I can be better than them.* I didn't have what they had yet, but I felt like it was attainable. And that lit a fire under my ass. Finally there was a chance to be the best at something. It was very exciting for me. When I was a skateboarder, my strategy was simple: figure out who was ahead of me, then pick them off, one by one. With the same passion I'd had as a teenager, I began the exact same attack on radio. That's been the mission ever since.

I WAS ON THE RADIO when my father died. After I started on Tony's show, I did a radio test thing in 2005 for my boss, Will Pendarvis, to try to get my own show on Faction, the same Sirius channel as Tony.

The story I told for that was from my father's wake. It was a pretty big accomplishment to tell that story, and not cry, and to find a funny way to tell it. I was very impressed by myself. Like I had already found my own little way to do things on the radio.

It was the story of the legendary Burnout King:

"After my father's funeral, we went back to my brother's house. This was essentially an after-party to a funeral. This was before we realized maybe we all drank too much—and one of the last times I was still really drinking. It was a man's party. We were drinking and smoking weed, and there were moto dudes there. We were out in the garage, and one of the moto dudes grabbed my brother's bike, put it up against the wall, opened it up into sixth gear, and pinned it in there. He did a massive burnout until the tire popped. We were all pretty excited about that.

"There was this friend of my dad's there. He's a Greek guy, but he's also Australian. There's a particular accent Greek guys have in Australia. You have to sort of imagine an Australian Dracula.

"So he talks to me. Everything he says is completely stone cold. 'Uh tell you wot, Jason. They call me the Buhn-Out King, mate. Uh'll do a special buhn-out, just for yuh' dad's passing, all right, mate?'

"Other guys keep doing burnouts with motor bikes, for a couple hours. Everyone's got their front brake on and we're in the garage and everyone's covered in carbon monoxide death smoke, and I'd almost forgotten all about the Burnout King when he comes and finds me and my brothers. We were all very intoxicated. We'd been drinking all day. That most definitely included the Burnout King. He tells us to come out to the front of the house. 'Uh've got something special for you, mate. Uh love yuh father. 'E wus a top bloke, mate.'

"So we go out there. While I respected and appreciated the gesture, I can't say I was excited about this. But it was nice of him to want to do something. The guy's put on a special tire, just for the occasion.

It's on his car. It's a suburban neighborhood, and by now it's dark out. But my dad never gave a fuck about the neighbors, and neither does this guy.

"He starts spinning the wheels. *Bem bem BEM.* Everyone's cheering. She starts smoking up. The dude opens the door, leaning out, checking out his work. He was very meticulous about his burnouts, you could tell.

"We're all standing around. It's burning, and there's smoke, and we can't believe how long it's going on for. And then, from inside the smoke, I can see this glow—a perfect orange donut, glowing inside his car. It's the metal in the brake. The crowd goes wild. And this guy's still got her pinned. We're going ballistic. The more smoke, and the more drama, the closer we all get to the car.

"And then there's fire. We all run toward the car, to be a part of the fire, and the smoke, and the glory of this burnout. I don't know what we were planning to do. Probably hoist the car, in respect to the Burnout King for the respect he had shown my father. It's like a Viking funeral.

"As we're running toward the car, yelling, the tire *explodes.* Fire and bits of rubber fly out, all over everybody. Flaming rubber is melting my flesh. Melting into me. The whole crew drops to the ground. Twenty dudes tucking and rolling.

"The Burnout King does not flinch. He's still pedal to the metal. I yell. 'Burnout King! Make it stop! Make it stop!' 'Nah, mate. You do nut know whut you ah doing.' The tire's flown off. The rim is sparking. His car is on fire. He does not care. It left a permanent burn stain on the side of his car.

"No one was actually harmed during this burnout, mind you. That's where I come from. You drink enough that, when fire and explosions happen, you run *toward* them. And everybody cheers.

"And this fucking champion—'Uh'm the Buhn-Out King, mate.

Uh'm one of the greatest Buhn-Out Kings that evuh lived.'—car on fire, metal on metal, *still* has it pinned. Flaming rubber still flying everywhere.

"This is the same car that he drives to work every day. Burnout King is apparently not a career that makes you a very wealthy man. Later on, I was like, 'Your car is pretty fucked up, Burnout King.' 'Uh tell you wot, mate. Yuh father was a sick cunt, mate. Uh loved him. Ah'd burn another car for him.'

"He fucked his car up good, burned the side of it up, and then he changed that tire the next morning and drove to work. Out of respect to my father. Love that guy."

I FEEL LIKE THE DEATHS of my father and my brother were an immediate connection to the fans. That's real life. People die. Fucking family members die. And if that's happened to you, and you hear some dude being honest about it on the radio, I feel like I've got you for the rest of my life.

For the longest time, I couldn't talk about certain things, because as soon as I tried, I started crying. I couldn't say the words. So I could never get it out. But right from the start, I found that on radio, they'll just come out. The emotions would still be in there, but not enough to stop me from telling the story. And at a high level of entertainment, too. I was almost a little bit disgusted with myself, that I could talk about my father's death, and sell it. That's what I'm doing. I'm boxing it up and I'm selling you my father's death. I almost hated myself for being able to explain it.

But I feel like that helped me, too. By the time my brother died in 2006, I had gotten my own nighttime show on Sirius, mainly just playing music, but talking, too. Everyone asked if I needed to take time off. But I just wanted to go to work. It was like therapy, being on the radio. Sometimes with therapists, you just talk. They don't even give you advice. You just tell your horrific story, to get it off your chest. I would do that every day.

Dyslexia was really embarrassing as a kid. Lots of things embarrassed me, majorly, like not being able to read, and like the time the tip of a tranny hooker's penis make contact with my asshole in Amsterdam. But now, all of a sudden, it was all just funny stuff to talk about on the radio. I'm a much more secure man now. I feel like talking about these experiences helps people. So for some reason, I can justify saying it on the air. And saying it helps *me* deal with it. Everybody wins.

Word started to spread. Really slowly, but still. At a Tony Hawk skate demo, somebody came up to me and said, "Man, I heard you on the radio!" And this was before I had a talk show. I was still a DJ. A lot of the time I was just doing fifteen-second talk breaks, introducing motherfucking AFI songs. As far as I was concerned, no one was listening. But people would be like, "I heard you talk about putting pizza in a cheeseburger. You're off your face." It was cool. You heard that on the radio? And you knew it was me?

When fans connected, then there was this new layer to it. It made me loyal to my listeners. Enough people called and said that they were moved by my stories. Or "I don't do heroin anymore." Or "I named my chinchilla after you." I remember those days. Where all of a sudden, people really care. I'm really helping people. And I've never been in that position before. I think deep down I'm a nice guy. I've always wanted to be one, anyway. And here were all these chances to help.

When I did that nighttime DJ show, the hours may have been a little weird for Andrea, but I let her know from the start that we had a game plan. I don't know if she actually believed me, but I told her I was going to be a huge success on the radio, and that both of us had to dig deep to make it happen. I would be there in the studio, with my arms raised, saying, "People! Listen! Everybody listen!" Trying to physically pull down a tractor beam of listeners from the sky. "Come with me!" And doing that would charge me up to say some shit. I came up with ideas and theories that even impressed myself.

I started talking about how the band Slipknot should make their own breakfast cereal for kids, and how I know my penis weighs six pounds soft, because one time I weighed it on a scale. And I spiraled off from there, into a place where I felt really comfortable. It was like a blanket. It made me feel warm. Just blathering on and on, and listening to myself like it wasn't me that was talking, and thinking, *Hey, that's pretty funny.* The part of me that was listening was entertained by the part of me that was talking. And then I was like a pig in mud.

There were some memorable early guests. Belladonna, a porn star, came in and put a light saber in her vagina. (A lot of the props in those days came from the toy section at Target, around the corner.) Yeah, sure, I've done some blow, and I've seen some hookers, but I've never seen a legitimate hard-core porn star stick things in her vagina. She was rough with it. She was bleeding at one point. I thought perhaps I should be concerned. She just shot me a look. Like, "What's the problem?" I felt like I was not worthy. What a job. The porn stuff was exciting, in the beginning. To have people perform, in the studio.

There was a lot of anxiety at first when guests came in. And not just the ones that fucked themselves with light sabers. But when I did good, I could get into someone's mind, and really get my guests to let their hair down and say something they didn't plan to say. I could tell when a guest was saying something to shock the listener. And I could tell when they said something crazy because I made them feel comfortable. After they let something slip, I could see it on their face like, *Ooh, maybe I shouldn't have said that.* But I got them to say it, before they caught it. I would be excited about that. I was in control. I would be amped on myself all night.

Those first guests that came in, I was absolutely nobody to them. Celebrities talk to radio show hosts pretty much against their will. When Jonathan Davis, the singer of Korn, came in, he was obviously not into me. This was a year or two into having my own show, when I had moved to afternoons and was basically just talking the whole time. Halfway through the interview, Jonathan was like, "Fuck, this is fun. I really like this guy." The singer of Korn really likes me? Because I'm funny and amusing? We bonded over how we're both raging alcoholics. And soon enough, he was talking about doing autopsies at a morgue, back before he sang for Korn. Talking about holding dead uteruses in the air. "This was the funnest interview I've ever had," he said. "You're gonna be huge." And off I trot home, feeling all jolly and successful.

One of the bad early ones was Johnny Rotten. That was also early in my afternoon show. Radio wants you to say, "Hey man, I've listened to all your albums." Even if you haven't. That's sort of expected of a DJ. So I had some notes. When Johnny Rotten was gonna be out on tour, and bullshit like that. Not believing in myself, that I don't need to do it the radio way. I can only do it my way.

He was being a dick. Of course. That's his thing. Let him have it. The other thing was the tough guy that was standing behind him. Rambo is his name. The two of them go everywhere together. Rambo was there sizing me up, greasing me the whole time. I remember thinking *You're fucking fifty, dude. You might have bottled a couple of people back in the day, but you do not have any weapons right now. Fuck you* and your tough ass. *I'll beat you, and your old man famous guy friend, too.* Before you know it, Rotten is all, "Interview's over," because I didn't know who was in the Sex Pistols these days. Honestly, I didn't know the Sex Pistols still existed.

Before he left, he said, "If you're gonna be in the game, at least try to be good at your job." I remember thinking that I had fucked up. I really didn't know anything about his band or the new tour or whatever. I'll beat myself up about things like that for days. I spent a long time thinking about that interview. And eventually I thought, you know what? From now on, when a guest comes in, I'm going to learn a couple of basics, just so I'm not completely disrespectful. But I'm also going to be asking you questions on behalf of everybody who *doesn't* know every last thing about you, you egotistical cunt. I learned a lot from that interview. I made a lot of adjustments. That's what I do now. "Who are you?" "What do you do?" "So, your song's a big hit, is it?" If a guest goes on Howard Stern, and Howard pronounces their name wrong, do they walk out? No. Stern doesn't watch your show, dude. Get over yourself. That was my angle, from then on.

I've been told I have the fastest-growing radio show in history, but that doesn't mean it hasn't been a struggle at times. Like when I was just a DJ, doing those fifteen-second intros on songs. I didn't even know how to work the board. Will, my boss, had to do it for me. It reminded me of my first job, working in the supermarket as a trolley boy. I remember thinking, *This is the bad part. This is the way it goes. This is paying your dues. I don't want to be here. I don't want to be told what to do and what to say.* And it wasn't just the radio part of it. My whole life had changed, fast. I would think, *I don't want to be in Los Angeles. I don't want to be sitting down. I don't want to be a nonskater. I don't want to grow up. I don't want to be married, and I don't want to have a kid.* It was tough. But I told myself, if I work hard at it, this will all work itself out. I was hoping that I could do it all over again. Do in radio what I had done in skateboarding. Because skateboarding wasn't that glamorous at the start either. But this time, I wasn't gonna blow it.

WHEN I STARTED DOING MY own show, my house was far away from the studio in Hollywood, and I couldn't afford to have an apartment near there. And the drives were so long. It was freaking me out. I was living in Temecula, and on Fridays after the show, thanks to Southern California traffic, sometimes the drive took me six hours. If I stopped at a Denny's to get out of the car for a bit, it could easily turn into an eight-hour day, just getting home from work. On top of maybe three hours driving in, and a four-hour show. It was crazy.

We didn't have much money, but I was always begging Andrea so I could get a hotel. I spent many a depressing evening at the cheapest hotel I could find, in the Koreatown area of L.A. My first night there, through the walls, I heard what I believe was potentially a girl being murdered. There was screaming, and then there were these muffling noises, and then when I came out, they were gone.

Then I found a place I could afford with my AAA discount. A Ramada. I think it was eighty bucks. The first time I ever stayed there, the roof was leaking into the shower. I called downstairs to tell them, and they said they'd give me a discount. They never came to check on it.

In a weird way, I liked it. I know, to a lot of people, being able to afford any hotel at all is a pretty big deal. But I'd already had a taste of the good life. It was funny to be stuck in that shitty situation. I told myself to remember it. *Leak all night,* I thought. *I'm gonna get out of here some day. I'm gonna work really hard at this radio thing, and I'm gonna look back on this and laugh.* Because I already thought I had radio figured out. I had a lot of belief in where my abilities were going to take me.

I'm a stressed-out, sleep-deprived, bleeding-ulcer, pooing-blood kind of guy, because I care about the fans. I worry about the show. I worry if I'm gonna have it again today. What if I just go flat? What if I do four hours of nothing funny whatsoever, and it's just gone? Skateboarding kind of happened that way.

It's the stress of my life, but then again it's the thing that makes me feel whole, besides my family. I need to be successful to feel whole. In my mind, I am a loser if I don't beat everybody and prove to everyone that the dude with dyslexia, who didn't pay attention in school, is successful. The void left behind from skateboarding, the massive hole, it's filled. I walk with confidence because of this show.

BACK IN THE DAY, EVERYTHING reminded me of skating. Everywhere I looked, everything I saw was an idea for a new trick. Any table I was sitting at, my fingers would be moving around, simulating possible new variations. And now, even though I do a million things every day, all my thoughts come back to the radio show. What can I do that's never been done before? Has anyone ever gotten bit by an anaconda on the air? No? Then get one in and let's do it (even though I *hate* snakes).

That was a big one for me. An eight-foot anaconda. The snake had been brought in the day before, and just seeing it fucked with me. I was really fucking scared. I could not control my body. I could not turn around and face the snake. I hid in the corner of my own studio. It was weird that something could make me do that. So I thought, *What if it bit me?* And then I realized, I was testing myself again. I was being dangerous again, after losing that edge at the end of my skateboarding career. Basically, I was back to being me again. I would love to hear about a guy like that on the radio. This guy is scared of snakes, and he just had an eight-foot anaconda bite him? Personally, I want to hear that radio show. I'm not getting out of the car until it fucking bites him.

Will Fedor Emelianenko—at one point quite possibly the most dangerous man in mixed martial arts—come by and kick me? Yes? Go get him. Then, fifteen minutes after the bit is done, I'm over it, and on to the next most humongous thing I can think of.

It's been cool to watch the show grow outside of the radio studio. Once or twice a year, thousands of people come out to my fight event, Ellismania. From the beginning, I've always been making stuff up on the radio. What about this? What if that happened? Ellismania is the natural offshoot of shooting the shit. We made up enough fight ideas on the air, and I had been talking about my own training so much, we eventually had to stop talking. We had to get out there, punch each other, and see what happened. I think a part of me just wanted to see if anyone was actually listening. If anyone would show up. And once they did, I was off into la-la land, dreaming up bigger and better things we could do.

The fans at Ellismania are what make it for me. Everybody laughing at the same time. Maybe even the guy that's currently being electrocuted and punched at the same time. We all laugh our asses off, and I feel like the leader of the fun pack. You definitely don't want to give that up. The way it's going, Ellismania may be the thing I'm most known for in the end.

The band is a big thing to me, too. We've had two bands, actually—Taintstick and Death! Death! Die! We've made the Billboard album charts. Death! Death! Die! had the number one metal song in America on iTunes. We also had the top five spots on the Canadian iTunes singles chart. Five different songs, all at the same time. Like a shitty-ass Beatles.

There are so many things I envisioned as a very young boy, and it's amazing how they have pretty much *all* come true. I may have had some bad times here and there, but the "I'm awesome" guy has never gone away. When I was a kid, cutting school and sitting by myself in an alley in Sandringham, or when I was the only vert skater at the ramp, or when I was drinking myself to sleep again while me and Rachel were breaking up, somewhere inside of me, there's a guy that has always been ready and waiting to rule the world at a moment's notice. I've always had visions of being ridiculously sweet. Many a night, for hours and hours, I imagined myself as the singer in a band. Somewhere in my deranged mind, even when I was a pro skater and it would have been ludicrous to have a side project as a metal singer, that dream was still in there. It was ridiculous when you think about it, but now it's true. The radio show has allowed me to get on a mike in front of a thousand people, and at least not get laughed off the stage.

Originally the point was to make fun of bands. Probably because of my envy toward people who *did* make it as musicians. Damn you, you good-looking bastards. I'm not a good singer, but I'm a good front guy. I'm fairly relaxed for a guy who's only performed live maybe twenty times. I just can't sing. That's all. With me being insecure, as I am, and being the singer and the head guy, that was stressful for me in the very beginning. Because the band can actually play, and then the lead singer is out of key. That made me kind of not want to be there. But now I look forward to it. I may drop out of key six or seven times a song, but the rest of the time I hold my own. I'm having fun. I'm watching the rest of the band. Watching the fans. To have the music thing happen in a way where I'm not gonna get carried away with it, and where it doesn't mean anything to me, it's kind of a relaxing thing. If I had pulled off the rock star thing before I was forty with two kids, it might have been different. But now, it's just fun. I am in a band where I can honestly say I don't care. I don't think any other band can say that.

I've also been a part of a couple of movies, too. Along with other people from my radio show, I made a horror movie, *The Woodsman,* at the same time we all did the *Death! Death! Die!* album. But the only reason I got to star in that is because I made it. You can also see me in *Paul Blart: Mall Cop.* I played the bald tattooed skater guy who gets his ass kicked by Kevin James in a tanning salon. It was fun being around that, but I wasn't really there as an actor. Mainly, the movie people just wanted a skateboarder for some action scenes.

I don't see myself being a famous actor. That's not my scene. I would like to be a comedic action hero, and if I get famous enough, I believe there will be an opportunity for that one role where I really go for it, in my own style. I just wish I didn't have to do so much radio while I was doing *Mall Cop.* We had a makeshift studio set up in an empty storefront, in the mall where we were filming, up in Massachusetts. At the end of every day, everyone would be like, "Let's go to dinner!" And I'd have to say, "No, thanks, but I think I'm gonna go hang out in this empty room by myself all night and talk into a microphone." But that was an experience. There have been a whole bunch of experiences.

My auntie sent me an e-mail recently. From Australia. She told me she's very proud of me, and that I'm the most successful Ellis that's ever been. I live in Beverly Hills, so I think as far as she's concerned, I'm on fire. I was reading her e-mail in the bathroom one morning. The light was broken, so I was reading on my phone, in the dark, and I started to cry. Just for a second. Because she's an Ellis, and she's related to Dad, and she said she's proud of me. That's enough.

That's all I ever wanted to do, was to make him proud.

HARDEN THE FUCK UP

In a roundabout sort of way, you could say I got into fighting because I was on the radio. For some reason I got into the habit of watching fights on YouTube when I was at the studio. I was just a music DJ at first, so there was a lot of time where I wasn't talking. That was the highlight, while the music was playing, sitting alone in the studio—watching kickboxing videos. Bob Sapp versus Ernesto Hoost comes to mind. Hammer fists, broken bones, people knocked unconscious. This was the craziest thing I've ever seen.

And then I went to Carey Hart and Pink's wedding. I was swimming on the beach there, and I remember thinking how fat I was. I hadn't skated in a while. I felt like such a sloth. So washed up. I had just recently quit drinking. I had a daughter. My father had passed away. I had moved to L.A. to try to become a radio warlord. A lot of stuff had happened. For the first time, I was completely cool with not having any drugs or alcohol at all.

I was at a Four Seasons on some island, and everyone was drinking the whole time, except Kit Cope, a four-time world Muay Thai champion who trained Pink and Carey. He had just had a fight with Kenny Florian in the UFC and had his shoulder pulled out. Kit didn't drink, and I became friends with him. He informed me that I was indeed overweight, and he invited me to come to Las Vegas to train with him. He took a photo of me with my shirt off and told me he would show me my fat ass again later, when I wasn't fat anymore.

My fat ass, when I first met Kit Cope.

We became friends really fast. He was actually one of the first real friends that I had outside of skateboarding. We were immediately really close. We called each other all the time. Borderline gay. I went to Vegas on weekends, stayed with Kit, and did kickboxing. He would kick the shit out of me. I would spar and wrestle. And he taught me jujitsu moves. I had a friend, somebody who wasn't a drug taker, and who lived a positive life. That was very impressive to me. That, and the fact that he was smaller than me, but he could beat the shit out of me.

Throughout most of my skating life, there was usually a guy I modeled myself on. The guy I was trying to be. Idols are goals. They're targets. Whoever I was modeling myself on at any given time, they inspired me to achieve. To become better at some skill I thought I needed.

Now Kit was kind of that guy. Don't get me wrong—I knew I could be a good fighter, but I never thought I was going to the UFC or anything like that. I was too old. Still, Kit was sober, and positive, and happy, and tough. He was the first nonskater that was such a role model in my adult life. I wanted to be a fighter, because of him.

After a while, obviously Andrea started to get bummed out that I was driving to Vegas every weekend. So I wanted to sign up for a gym closer to home. We had just bought the house in Temecula, which is inland from San Diego. I thought I would live down there and ride moto all the time. But then I broke my wrist skating, and I went to a doctor who turned out to also be the MMA fighter Dan Henderson's doctor. From hanging out with Kit, I had seen a bunch more fights, so I knew all about Dan and the Axe Murderer, Wanderlei Silva, fighting each other. Possibly one of the greatest fights ever. From this doctor I found out that Dan had a gym right by my house.

By the time I went to the gym, I had already been on the "Bubba the Love Sponge Show," which at that time was on Howard Stern's

Sirius channel. Bubba had his own octagon, and some drama had started between me and him. He wanted to fight me, so I said I would. These guys were on Howard's channel. This was a chance to get my foot in the door with the big dudes.

This was four or five years ago. I'm still waiting for that fight. But at the time, I thought it was really going down. So as soon as I started training, in my mind I was training for a fight. I became friends with Ryan Parsons, who was the trainer at Dan's gym, Team Quest. Ryan wanted to learn how to skate, so we made a deal where we would train each other. He helped me a lot with the stress of sobriety. He was another one of my first nonskateboarding friends.

Pretty much from the start, within a month, I was training with the team. The first thing I did was spar with Thierry Sokoudjou. Sokoudjou had just knocked somebody unconscious in Pride. He was a prodigy. He looked like the Predator. He was easily the most shredded human being I've ever seen in my life. He was telling me to punch him in the face, and then congratulating me whenever I landed a good one. I've known some tough dudes, but I remember thinking, *Who are these people?* I became friends with Dan Henderson. And also with Jason "Mayhem" Miller, who started coming on my radio show all the time.

A long time ago, when me and Mayhem became friends, I said, "When I grow up, I wanna be just like you." And he said, "When I grow up, I wanna be just like you, Ellis." I copy from him, and he copies from me. I'm a shitty MMA fighter who's really funny, and he's pretty funny, plus he's one of the greatest MMA fighters of all time. We'd always joke about that. I think Mayhem knows that he's more talented than just as a fighter. I think he believes that when fighting ends, there's room for him in entertainment. He does have a gift.

He's taught me millions of things. He taught me to catch jabs with my forehead. We've spent hours together, jabbing each other in the head. He was the first person to break my nose. One time, I remember, he had some pills he was supposed to take to not be crazy, and he didn't have them with him, so I was like, "Why don't we go to the gym and spar, and you can just let it out there?" He was into that. I didn't realize what I was signing myself up for. He was angry. He ended up breaking my nose and giving me a black eye. He actually kind of switched me off for a second. Then I went back to his apartment, and Ryan Parsons and King Mo, another fighter, were there, and they both started laughing. All Mayhem said was, "He wanted me to do it." I didn't even realize how bad I looked until I saw myself in the mirror. That's when I realized how stupid I was. Still, I don't regret it. It was awesome to me to be in the middle of something like that. I loved it. It was an honor to be punched by someone so legendary.

It hurts getting hit, but there's this instant gratification that comes with the pain. There's always been a part of me that thrives on pain. I love getting punched in the face. That may sound sick, but as a skateboarder, I've been in some kind of pain or another for years. I've got arthritis that isn't gonna go away. To me, pain means you're pushing your body to give you everything its got. It means that you're alive. Nothing gets me out of my own head more than somebody punching me in the face. You really just forget about everything else in the world. I'm not trying to be the best fighter in the world. I'm just trying to feed the monster. And the monster wants carnage. That's what makes me happy.

The weird thing is, I have always had an aversion to inflicting pain. I've never been a street fighter. Ever. I saw my dad do it too many times. But MMA is a sport. When I started training, I wasn't trying to beat people up. I got into it to get healthy. To get into shape. Along the way, though, it's definitely helped me face that fear. Fuck, maybe even conquer it.

I got addicted to training. I was all in, instantly. I remember call-ing Andrea all the time, on the way home from the gym, telling her about whatever new move I had just learned. That became all I cared about. Fighting was the thing that helped me to move on, and to ease the pain and not be mind-fucked about not being a professional skateboarder anymore. I started to get obsessed with learning fight-ing tricks. Just like I used to learn skating tricks. I really felt like I was a part of something. It was like starting from scratch all over again.

And then there was the whole nutrition element. All these other sober people telling me what was good for me and what was bad for me. I saw my body start to change. I went from being a professional skateboarder to the sloth I was at the end of my career, and now sud-denly I was fitter than I had ever been in my life. At thirty-five years old. That lit a fire under my ass.

Unfortunately, while my body was getting stronger, my mind still needed work. After my brother passed away, I wasn't getting drunk anymore, but I might still have a couple of glasses of red wine. Or smoke my blunts.

I kept doing the radio show every day, but more and more, my mind would find its way to extremely dark places. I might be inter-viewing Bret Michaels from Poison about whether or not he has herpes, but my mind would be on this constant loop of evilness. My father dying. And then my brother dying. And then, when am I going to die? Am I having a heart attack *right now?* And what about all of the terrible things that could be happening in the world, *right this second?* Was Bret Michaels, and everyone, everywhere else, *about to fucking die?!* Just the darkest shit imaginable.

One morning I woke up, and I had a little shortness of breath. I told Andrea in the shower. I came into the radio studio, but I felt flat and depressed and weak, like my heart wasn't even beating. I went to the doctor. He told me he had to do some tests. He also told me that I was self-medicating myself, and making it worse. I wasn't getting shitfaced anymore, but he told me I had to stop the weed and the drinking completely. So that's when I finally did.

Being a husband and a father had pushed me in that direction. Having a second chance at glory with the radio show did, too. But there's nothing like a doctor saying you might die to make you cut the shit for good.

Unfortunately, the anxiety continued. Another doctor told me I needed to eliminate strenuous activity. Which is fine, except . . . do you know who you're talking to? You might as well just kill me now.

I had more panic attacks on the air. Once I needed to stop the show early and go to the hospital. Next thing I know, I was in the middle of that whole hospital scene, like on TV. Lying in the bed. The machine going *beep beep beep*. Medical people talking to each other about how my heart was beating a certain way, and I was going into a state of whatever. I remember looking at the ceiling of the hospital.

"God," I said. "Or Dad. If anybody up there is in charge of this bullshit, can you please make this stop?"

I got all these pills to sedate me and slow my heart down. I remember being in the shower at the hospital with the IV in my veins, crying, because I would never skate again. It's funny how skating was still the biggest loss to me. And I hadn't skated for ages. But to never skate again just seemed so sad.

There were more tests. More doctors. More anxiety. More dark moments where I was absolutely sure I was going to die, and that the entire world might well go down with me. Finally, I needed to take my friend, Devlyn Steele, with me to the doctor. He's a life coach. He runs a website called Tools to Life, and he's one of the more sane people I know. The doctor says, "You don't have heart disease." And Devlyn is standing next to me, literally saying, "Can you hear what the doctor is saying to you, Jason? You are not going to die." Devlyn had introduced me to another doctor who gave me pills for anxiety. I was taking them, but just to humor Devlyn. I was really thinking, *You idiot. I have heart disease. I'm going to have a heart attack and die. Anxiety pills are not gonna stop that.* But the heart specialist was now telling me that the anxiety pills were good for me. And again, Devlyn is there, like a translator, trying to penetrate my mind, saying, "Do you hear the doctor, Jason? The anxiety pills are what you need."

I was still going to the gym a lot. Even if it was freaking me out to do it, I'm not the kind of person that can just sit on the couch all day and be cool with that. Mayhem Miller and our friend Ryo Chonan took to me to Justin Fortune's boxing gym in Hollywood. Justin is Australian, and he was supposed to be the man to make your hands good. He fought Lennox Lewis once. And he gave him a pretty good fight, too. I remember doing pad work with Justin. "You've got a lot to learn," he said. "But we can fix you." By that point I got rid of my house and had an apartment near the radio studio. This meant I could actually see my family, rather than spending my entire life on the radio and in my car. It also meant I could go to Fortune's all the time. Me and Justin became instant friends. It was a total dad thing. Justin is just like my dad. Cold. A tough cunt.

He trained me to be a boxer. He told me I had heavy hands. He taught me this right hook and told me to concentrate on the way it felt when I landed it. "You feel that?" he said. "Anybody you touch with that, they go to sleep. Doesn't matter who it is. I train pro fighters. You touch any one of them with that, they go out." This was tremendously exciting news.

Justin wanted to get me an amateur boxing fight. There was three months of training and diet and plios and doing stuff in an altitude room and all that. Over the course of the three months, I could see my hands get faster. I could even hear the sound getting faster when I hit pads or hit the bag.

The boxing fight was actually the best fight I've had, because Justin was there for it. He's such a good trainer; he made me feel at ease. I was so comfortable in the dressing room. So happy.

Some skateboarders came in. Bucky Lasek was giving me his expert advice on what I should do in the ring. I could tell he was shit-faced, so I humored him. Pierre-Luc and Matthias picked up a pair of gloves. Also shitfaced. Both of them put on one glove, and next thing you know, someone got punched in the head, and their head ricocheted off the dressing room wall. I forget which of those two idiots it was.

I've never been so sober and so fit in my life. And yet I'm washed up, and these guys are rich professional skateboarders?

Fuck, did I blow it.

The day before the fight, I saw my opponent, and he was bigger than me. He'd been training for four years, versus my three months. But Justin wasn't impressed. "That guy's fucking nose is dead straight. He can't fight for shit." I didn't know what he meant. "Anyone who has a straight nose can't fucking fight. Trust me, you'll fucking kill him." The idea was, if you'd really been training for four years—the right way—you would have taken a few shots that would have rearranged your nose a bit. I figured Justin knew what he was talking about. And that took away the fear.

The fight lasted ninety seconds.

Then he went to sleep.

I just mowed through the guy. I barely even knew what happened. I remember Justin trying to take my gloves off. I was like, "What are you doing?" Justin looked at me like I was crazy. He pointed at my opponent, who was still facedown on the canvas. It was such a proud moment. Kit Cope was in my corner. Ryan Parsons was there. It was in front of Tony Hawk and all these other people. That was a Cinderella story.

THEN RYAN SHECKLER ASKED ME to fight at his charity event in 2009. MMA. Ryan Parsons had been planning to take me to Tijuana for my first MMA fight, to face some random Mexican dude. But this was way better. This was in L.A., at the House of Blues.

But the anxiety didn't go away after the boxing match. It actually got worse. The MMA fight was way more cardio oriented. Plus the boxing fight was amateur—this one was pro. I thought I was going to have a heart attack training, again. I know that sounds crazy. But this is me we're talking about. It didn't have to make sense.

Obviously, a lot of it was mental. I think at that point I had been beaten into this dark place. Good things were starting to happen for me, and in my mind, if good things happen to me, that just means that death is around the corner. The world's about to end. Because that's my fucking track record. As soon as things might get good, somebody's probably going to die. And it's probably going to be me. I mean, how have I avoided it this far? I'm thinking, *Your father and your brother are gone—you* have *to be next.*

I powered through it as best I could. When my dad died, I remember being really scared of pedaling on an exercise bike. Because my dad died pedaling up that mountain. I still feel like my life is bound to follow in his footsteps. The day I go from fifty-two to turning fifty-three, like he was about to, I guarantee you I'm going to need some Valiums. But I remember pedaling on an exercise bike with headphones on, and dealing with it. Talking to myself. *I'm gonna pedal all the time, so that I'm not him.*

Once I got past pedaling and not having a heart attack in the process, I would go to the gym and really work out. I would do forty minutes pedaling a bike like a fucking maniac, just for a warm-up. I had to get new headphones, because I would sweat so hard my old ones would fall out of my ears, and I would get so pissed because I was in such a zone with whatever song I was listening to.

I remember listening to Sepultura and running on the beach. I could never handle running when I was younger. I remember a couple times, for contests, getting amped and going out there to try it, and then telling myself, *Man, running is stupid.* It was the monotony. Back then, my brain needed to jump an obstacle. Something. Anything. Twenty minutes of jogging was like being on a plane for twenty hours. But now I had the bug. I wanted to be fitter and better, and train more.

Cutting weight alone was a massive struggle. For breakfast, I would have half a bowl of oatmeal and half a sweet potato. Grilled chicken breast and veggies for lunch. Maybe some fish for dinner. Everything was tasteless. No seasoning. And all while burning crazy calories at the gym. The highlight of the day was having a protein shake after training, because it had sugar. Meaning it actually tasted like something. I lost over twenty pounds for my fight.

I was training with pros. Everyone I trained with was famous. I never landed anything. I never took anybody down. I didn't win one time. Every day, I just got the shit beat out of me, and then I would get pissed, and then Mayhem and all those guys would say, "Take it, bitch."

I became friends with a guy who had been on *The Ultimate Fighter.* I started to be able to outrun him. And then one time, when Ryan Parsons was doing circuit training with me and that guy, we stayed after for a chin-up contest. I've got a massive ass and little arms, so chin-ups are really hard for me. At the very end, Ryan told us to hold the bar at eye level and stay there. First one to quit loses. And Ryan is barking at me and this dude. Asking the fighter, "Are you going to lose to a fucking skateboarder?" And then on to me. "Ellis, what do you think? You're a fucking fighter?" I was in by then. Hook line and sinker. I was spitting, snotting, holding on with everything I had.

And right at the last second, before I gave in, I discovered that if I let my brain go somewhere else, then I could not feel anything. There is a place inside my mind where the pain doesn't stop me anymore. I could keep holding on. I could just stay there. It was a massive discovery.

Then . . . I thought about it too much, and I fucked myself. Me and the other guy dropped at the exact same time. We tied.

But I had learned, in that moment, that my mind could allow me to work through more pain than I thought I could endure.

IN ORDER TO GET CERTIFIED for a pro MMA bout, they tested me for my professional fighter's license. They test your eyes, your brain, everything. They tested my cardio, and when they did the test, the machine wasn't working. They said it was a malfunction. The machine's fault. But I was sure they were wrong. This was it—they were finally going to figure out that I have heart disease, and then they weren't going to let me fight. Even after Devlyn Steele standing there with me in the doctor's office, asking me if I was hearing what the doctor was saying, I just couldn't believe that I might be okay.

I passed the test. Good to go. But then, the day before the fight, the athletic commission wouldn't sanction my opponent. The asshole didn't pass *his* tests. So instead, they replaced him with a guy who'd already had three pro fights. Everybody tried to tell me it would be fine, but I knew we were dealing with a professional fight promoter, and a fight promoter doesn't give a shit what happens to me.

I had trained as hard as I possibly could. Along the way, I broke something in my hand, so my hand was fucked for a while, but I didn't cheat one time. No dairy. No nothing. I was on an insane diet for two straight months, while training every day *and* doing a radio show. I did everything exactly the way you're supposed to. I've never been that disciplined. I would never say that discipline is a skill that I possess. So in a way, I felt like I had already won. Even before the fight, I had a confidence that I knew wasn't going away. I had done it. I weighed 183 pounds, all the way down from 205. When I stepped on that scale, I saw every ab in my stomach. That had never happened before. I'm not one of those guys who just gets a six-pack. It was awesome to be there. To have gone that far.

UNTIL CRUNCH TIME, ON THE night of the fight, I didn't even think about the fact that all of skateboarding was gonna be there. It was a Ryan Sheckler event, after all. Ryan was there backstage, saying "Ellismate, you're gonna do it!" I saw Sal Masekela in the dressing room. I never saw any of these people anymore. I'd been out of that world for so long. Mayhem and Ryan and King Mo, that was my family now. We trained together. We talked about girlfriend problems together. We were tight. I had these people in my corner. Some drunk skateboard dudes saw me, and got in my face. "What's up, Ellis!" And all of a sudden, all I could think was, *Who the fuck are you guys?*

Justin Fortune couldn't be there. He had to go corner a professional boxer that same night. That threw a huge spanner in it for me. He was my confidence. He was my security. I know Ryan knows what he's doing, but I trust Justin more. Like I said, Justin's a tough cunt from Australia. Just like my dad. I think I just wanted some of that in my corner. Plus, I know Mayhem and Mo love me, but I'm a boxer. I knew I was going to box this dude. And my boxing trainer wasn't there.

I was nervous. In the locker room, Mayhem was like, "You've done it, dude. You did the training. I'm fucking proud of you." Mo was like a hyper little kid. He was telling me about how you only get one first fight, and how jealous he was of me. He kept saying, "You're gonna have so much fun!" I looked at him like he was sick. Because I felt terrible.

Kit Cope was the main event, right after me. We were in the dressing room together, and he was getting nervous for his fight, and he smiled at me. Like, how hilarious is this that we're both here right now? "Get out there and do it," he said. It was pretty funny. This guy taught me how to throw my first punch, how to kick, how to jump rope, how to lift weights. Everything.

Before I came out, Mo had been folding up my gloves and then slamming the door on them, over and over, wearing them in. Like a guru sharing a little pro secret. He wore the padding down to nothing. I put them on, and I felt them, and I realized, *If I catch you with this, you're unconscious.* And I'm assuming my opponent's guys are on the other side, doing the same thing. This was so fucking lethal, what we were doing. This is fucking crazy.

It was time to turn on the insanity.

WHEN THE TIME CAME, I stood behind the curtain. They were playing my Metallica song. I had envisioned this moment a million times. This song, and how I would feel. The energy rushing through me. My dad, and my brother. The skateboarding world. They were all there with me.

Standing behind the curtain, I started punching myself in the face. Trying to warm my face up. I thought we were going to stand up and bang, so I wanted to get my head ready to get punched. Nobody told me to do it. I would never do it again. It didn't work at all. I started rocking myself. I was so amped, and the gloves were so nonexistent, I almost knocked myself out before the fighting started.

And then I started feeling really lethargic. I have been told that's called an adrenaline dump. Your body gets so amped up, it crashes.

And then the curtain went up.

That music always gets to me. "Ecstasy of Gold" by Metallica. I walked to the ring, with all these skateboard dudes yelling my name. Other than Ryan and Sal, I hadn't really seen anybody, because I had been in the back the whole time. I forgot where I was. There were all these dudes that are cool and relevant. The current generation. I didn't even know that they knew who I was.

I felt like I was saying good-bye to skateboarding, right then and there. It was a cool world. A cool scene. And it's moving on without me. But right here, right now, they all think I'm cool again. One more time. That wasn't going to happen for me on a skateboard ever again. But I got the feeling that people wanted me to win because of what I've done in skateboarding. It was like they were telling me, "You are one of us." It felt good, because I didn't really feel like I was anymore.

It was a great send-off. Thanks, everybody.

I WAS REALLY NERVOUS IN that cage. I remember hugging Mayhem. I was living the dream, just like I've seen in so many videos.

You hugged your team just before you walk into the cage, just like a real fighter. That's what I wanted from this. Just to be a real fighter.

And I looked over at my opponent. Psychologically, at my boxing fight, the other guy had the upper hand. But this time, come fight night, I had snapped. I looked at him and thought, *I'm gonna fucking kill you, dude.* Justin Fortune got in my head. "Don't touch gloves. Fuck this cunt. Fucking kill this cunt. He wants to fucking kill you." So I had convinced myself to just go crazy.

My opponent looked at the ref, holding his hand up like, *We should touch gloves. Okay, fine,* I thought. *I'll touch your fucking glove.* But I remember touching gloves and thinking, *This guy is scared of me.* The roles had been reversed. The crowd was there to watch me kill this dude. That was my train of thought. He was scared as fuck. That was reassuring. But then again, I was incredibly nervous, too.

I really had no game plan at all. It all went out the window. I made every rookie mistake possible. He kicked, and I ran toward him without punching, and I caught him at the cage, and I heard Mayhem yelling, "Spin off the cage!" And after I did that, I just stood there. I didn't do anything. I waited for my opponent to do something. I didn't throw down, or elbow. Everything I had trained for, I completely forgot. I couldn't sleep the night after my fight. I spent the whole night thinking, regretting everything I had done.

All of a sudden he threw me on the ground. I was on my back straightaway, and he had a triangle on my body, trying to punch me in the side of the head. That's when I realized that I was in the fight. That's when I woke up.

I dodged a bullet. Up until that point, I could've gotten knocked out. I wasn't even looking. I was so nervous. When he punched me in the head the first time, that's when it hit me. I thought, *Look, dude, you're gonna lose this fight.*

And that was not gonna happen.

I needed some advice. Mayhem had been yelling the whole time, and now, it occurred to me it might be a good idea to listen.

He was still yelling. "Roll! Roll! Roll!" So I rolled. I remember Ryan talking to me about wrist control. "If you've got a wrist, he can't finish you." So I had both hands on one of his wrists, while he was punching me in the head. I rolled one way and then another way and then I rolled right into a mount. He had the mount for a second, and as soon as I felt that, I rolled the other way.

And then he tried to slip into an arm bar. All these lessons that had been drilled into my brain started coming back to me. When he went for the arm bar, I saw it coming. I told myself there was no way he was getting it. That I was way stronger than this dude.

I told myself, if he pulls my arm, and if he breaks something, I have to hide it. I'm not trying to brag, but I can honestly say, I knew I wasn't going to tap. It was too soon. I had to fucking get him. I decided, if he tries to break something, knock him out while he's breaking it.

I got on top of him. Whew. I punched him once in the stomach, and then I fell on him. Right then and there, I felt him give up. He put so much into the triangle and the arm bar, he had gassed. So I was on top of him, and he was on his back. His feet were over his head. I was able to look at him between his legs and I could see fear in his eyes.

I really wasn't worried anymore. I got side control. I started kneeing him, and elbowing him, and switching them up, so he couldn't block one or the other. He was wincing a lot.

When we got up from the first round, I was so tired. In the corner, Ryan told me, "He's gonna kick you in the leg again. As soon as you see that leg leave the ground, throw a straight right hand."

The second round is when I got my wind back. That's when all the training paid off. As soon as he threw that kick, I threw my right hand. It just skimmed him. But then a left hand did a bit of damage. I put him on the ground and was on top of him. I kneed him and punched him and I knew he was giving up.

I started to get cocky. He was looking for a way out. I was confident enough to really try to posture up and knock him out. As soon as I postured up, he slipped off to the side and put his head on the side of my rib cage. I feel like he kind of gave it to me. Right there, if he'd stayed down, I was going to rain on his face. He gave me his head, and as soon as I pulled on it, he tapped. I was like, *Already? Are you kidding me?*

The ref touched me, and then straightaway I was going for the cage. Colin McKay was already in there with me. He wasn't allowed to be there, but, well, he always pulls off shit like that. He's a Red Dragon.

Colin got in my way. I was so tired, his leg almost blocked me. I almost fell off the cage.

But then I did exactly what I had seen in my mind. I got up on the cage and pointed at the ceiling. *Look at me, Dad,* I thought. *I did it. You didn't think I could do that.*

This is what I had wanted. I wanted to train, and almost die, and give it everything I've got, and then get it all out. All of my fucking rage. My arm was raised. I had faced myself, the only person in the room I truly felt I had anything to prove to.

And that day, at least, I won.

ACKNOWLEDGMENTS

I wanna thank Mike Tully for writing this book and for being a good friend. Josh Richmond, Devlyn Steele, Ryan Parsons, Jason "Mayhem" Miller, Will Pendarvis, Kevin Zinger, Ken and Cindy Brown, Ken and Lucy Block, Ellisfam, Justin Fortune, MMA, Chad Reed, Christian Hand, Bryan Cullen, Mike Cechnicki, Grimey RIP, my dog Fifty, God, Shane Carwin, Howard Stern, Lee Ellis, Marn Ellis, skateboarding, Benji Madden, Moses, Sluggo, and Colin, Kit Cope, Carey Hart, Lance Mountain, Ryan Steely, Courtney Berman, Mike O'Meally, Dan Swinmurn, Mike Blabac, Sal Masekela, Metallica, Tony Hawk, Andrea, Devin, and Tiger Ellis.